Europe Without Frontiers

Europe Without Frontiers

Socialists on the Future of the European Economic Community

Neil Kinnock
Willy Claes
Jacques Delors
Laurent Fabius
Felipe Gonzalez
Wim Kok
Hans Jochen Vogel
Piet Dankert, editor
Ad Kooyman, editor

Mansell Publishing for Cassell
London and New York

First published 1989 in the English language by
Mansell Publishing Limited for Cassell
Artillery House, Artillery Row, London SW1P 1RT, England
125 East 23rd Street, Suite 300, New York 10010, U.S.A.

© 1989 Van Gorcum & Comp. B.V., P.B. 43, 9400 AA Assen, The Netherlands

This is the first title in the *Mansell for Cassell* series, *Towards Tomorrow*.

British Library Cataloguing in Publication Data

Europe without frontiers: Socialists on the future of the European Economic
Community.
1. European community. Socialism
I. Dankert, Piet II. Kooyman, Ad
335'.0094

ISBN 0-304-31810-8 paper
ISBN 0-304-31842-6 cased

Library of Congress Cataloging-in-Publication Data

Europe without frontiers: Socialists on the future of the European Economic
Community/edited by Piet Dankert and Ad Kooyman.
000 p.   cm. -- (Towards tomorrow)
ISBN 0-304-31810-8 paperback. ISBN 0-304-31842-6 cased.
1. European Economic Community countries - Economic conditions.
2. Economic forecasting - European Economic Community countries.
3. European Economic Community countries - Economic policy
4. Europe - Economic integration.
5. Socialism - European Economic Community countries.
I. Dankert, Piet.
II. Kooyman, Ad.
III. Series.
HC241.2.E8163   1989
337.1'42--dc20

Illustration on the cover: Lonius
Printed in The Netherlands by Van Gorcum

Contents

Preface

The future of social democracy has been questioned in recent years. There has been much talk of a new approach, the need to adapt. The discussion has frequently ignored the enormous challenge facing social democracy in the next few years: the European internal market of 1992.

Social Democrats have long been ambivalent in their attitude towards the European Community. Their great political success in the second half of the twentieth century – the welfare state – was achieved within the national context. The European Community with its additional economic growth provided the financial resources for this achievement, but the link between the EC and the welfare state was seldom made.

Nor was there any need to do so: the process of European unity rapidly came to a standstill. From the mid 1960s in particular until the early 1980s the EC tended to be the victim of crisis rather than the impetus for integration. Initial enthusiasm gave way to the threat of disintegration. In many areas Japan took over from divided Europe. Businessmen woke up with a start, as did European politicians. 1992 was their magic formula for a concerted effort. Not planning, but the market, would help to get us all back on our feet. Deregulation and privatization became the new slogans.

This book is about socialism and a Europe without frontiers. For the sake of jobs and prosperity and because of their own powerlessness, at the national level, to control an increasingly international economy, the Social Democratic and Socialist parties in the EC have accepted 1992. But we want more. In Europe, too, a compromise must be found between the state and society, capital and labour and – last but not least – between economic growth and the environment.

In this book leading Social Democrats from various EC Member States discuss the implications of 1992. They tackle it from very different angles and reach different conclusions. The problems they identify are often the same ones. They all discuss in depth the social dimension of a Europe without frontiers, the problem of the distribution of wealth and prosperity, the new multinationals, the need for new forms of consultation and codetermination for workers and what from the new 'economic order' will take and what its priorities should be. This book does not claim to have tailor-made solutions for the Europe of 1992. That would be impossible. The problems are too complex and future political developments too uncertain.

Lasting solutions will need to be found in the coming years in the light of the disposition of political forces and the development of the internal market. This book is intended to fuel the debate on these issues.

Ad Kooyman
Piet Dankert

Facing the future of the European Community

Neil Kinnock
Leader of the Labour Party (England)

It has been clear for a long time now that the European Community has fulfilled few of the aspirations of its original architects and British membership has brought little of the benefit anticipated by its advocates. The inefficient and unjust Common Agricultural Policy has continued to soak up resources. The Community has been singularly ineffective in improving Europe's world market share, or in mitigating the economic domination of multinational corporations – many of which owe no allegiance to any European interest. The regular 'summits' of EC Leaders have been remarkable for their failure to address the central issues of European economic and social performance. Unemployment, North-South relations, technological and scientific co-operation have been the stuff of communique footnotes rather than of primary strategy. And meanwhile the economic decline of the United Kingdom – especially outside the South-East of England – has gone on despite the oil.

Now – and until 1992 – the preoccupying issue is and will be the obsessive drive to a Single European Market. Among the progressive forces in the Community there are those who identify it as the new 'Europeanist' development, the mark of 'European' political commitment. Others, motivated by less laudable ideals, employ the same rhetoric but seek the change for

1

reasons that have everything to do with securing domination by the market and nothing to do with achieving the development of community. Indeed some people, seeing the vocabulary of the Single Market discussions liberally salted with words like 'de-regulation', make the assumption that the Market will exclusively and inevitably be an open space for the operation of New Right economics.

A former adviser to Mrs Thatcher and now the new Commission Secretary General, David Williamson has, for instance, referred to the Thatcherite view of 1992 as 'rather a heavy concentration on the internal market as a cash-register operation'. There are others too, who already understand that if the Single Market was to mean nothing other than a big-finance free-for-all it would be a social, industrial and environmental catastrophe.

Understanding that as we do, we have to ensure that democratic socialists take every opportunity in every member country to initiate policies that will steer the European economy in productive and socially just directions, bearing in mind the plain fact that single markets have always existed in national economies without preventing socialists from pursuing progressive policies. Every one of our Movements in every one of our countries has, by a variety of means – varying from public ownership to consumer protection legislation and from minimum labour standards to environmental health controls – made constant efforts to civilize the operation of markets and to make economic activity compatible with human security.

In the philosophy of the nineteenth century economic liberals, and in the policies of their successors, the 'New Right' of our age, the kinds of safeguards our Movements have achieved are impediments to the 'great adventure' of market capitalism. To everyone else they are necessary limitations to the excesses and abuse that follow from the inevitable tendency of that system to put profit before people. In so many respects, the relative comfort and safety of modern life is due to the success achieved by socialists and others who realise that life is too important to be

2

left to the dictates of demand and supply. That is the spirit in which we must approach the new scale of market operation. Our failure to be assertive about the just and productive course that the Community must take would mean unimpeded movement to the complete economic and political domination of Western Europe by market power – with all of the effects on civil rights, environmental conditions, individual opportunities and collective provision which that implies. That is the central reason why we have to retain and gain the powers necessary to propel Europe in the direction of 'Community' as well as ensuring that it is a Market for the people and not against them.

It is therefore surely right to emphasize that any significant change, such as the Single Market, should be judged by its likely impact upon the consumers and workers of the Community, a requirement of justice and of efficiency. It is a demand that democratic socialists have always made and must always make. Throughout history, socialists have argued for the need to prevent the hardship, exploitation and waste which can result from the operation of unregulated markets. Those arguments have been produced by experience, not by abstract theorizing. The evidence of abuse was manifest long before the response was assembled. It is those considerations which must apply now as the European Community is turned into a Single European Market. There should be no confusion.

The 1992 process is not about mopping up petty and outdated restrictions or in promoting international co-operation. The purpose of the process is the removal of many of the protections for consumers, citizens and workers which have been built up by national Parliaments over decades, and which are seen as 'rigidities' impeding market operations. In these circumstances it is vital to highlight the need for Europe to act cohesively in seeking a restructuring of world economic, trade and financial relations, in order to tackle the problems of the developing countries and to stimulate sustained economic growth across Europe, including those nations and regions which will otherwise be abandoned and excluded from prosperity.

3

Detailed arguments for action need to be made and detailed proposals need to be formulated. That is the job which now deserves our universal attention. That is the point of view from which the specific measures in the Single Market programme must be judged.

Most of those 300 or so specific measures are said to be aimed at overcoming cost disadvantages which prevent efficient use of productive resources. According to the Commission, these could represent as much as 6 per cent of Community GDP, although this estimate is the most optimistic and does rely upon some rather improbable calculations. More important is the assumption that if costs are reduced by 6 per cent, then GDP will necessarily increase by an equivalent amount. Such an assumption is glib and superficial.

For that neat transfer to happen, there would have to be a costless re-allocation of resources, a prospect that is certainly belied by British experience and indeed by all reality. Too much of the rhetoric about the single market has assumed that it is an end in itself. It is not, it cannot be.

The reality is that a whole range of complementary policies need to be put in place to make it work for the peoples of the Community. And many of those policies – such as a co-ordinated growth strategy – ought to be implemented irrespective of the single market. Governments and the Community itself need to act to ensure that the manifest weaknesses of an uncontrolled market are combatted. For example, both national governments and the Community as a whole have vital roles to play in addressing; the social upheaval that has been caused and could be intensified by migration towards the centre of Europe; the transformation of existing systems of wage bargaining; the increasing difficulty likely to be experienced by enterprises – especially medium and small sized businesses – seeking capital in the peripheral areas of the Community; the implications of removing public spending as a means of promoting social policy; and the intensification of mergers and takeovers and the way in which that can disrupt or deter sustained investment in, for instance,

4

research and development, training and marketing as companies maximize profits to persuade stockholders from accepting bids from predators.

The British government – unlike those of other European countries whatever their political complexion – has been singularly inactive in protecting British interests and ensuring that Britain is properly prepared, both to take advantage of such economic opportunities as the new market arrangements offer, and to combat the adverse effects. Just as other national Governments have been active in pursuing the interests of their peoples, so too the people of Britain need action from the British Government which will ensure that their interests are safeguarded in that new market.

With that in mind, I want to set out some of the major considerations on which the approach of the British Labour Party will be based. First, and most important, the drive to a Single Market cannot and must not be an end in itself. We, as Socialists, must establish our own vision for Europe up to and beyond 1992. Second, we must look at the proposals in the 1985 Commission White Paper as a package. None of us will completely agree with all of the 300 original proposals. But I am sure that we would regard many of them – particularly those dealing with physical and technical barriers – as sensible measures to remove unnecessary obstacles to the movement of goods, capital and people across borders. The Commission must take steps to ensure that any cost reductions which do follow from reduction of the barriers within the Community are directed towards economic expansion and growth. Third, the drive to a Single European Market will tend to lead to the reinforcement of existing imbalances in the European economy, concentrating industry, employment and prosperity in those parts of Europe where they are already strongest and increasing the potential for rapid and destabilizing capital movements. The claim that the benefits of the single market will help the declining regions is based on an economic theory which holds that enterprises, with perfect knowledge and seeking optimum profit, can and do

5

relocate to regions where factors of production, such as land and labour, are cheaper than elsewhere. Such theories are safe in textbooks and nowhere else. No credibility should or can be given to them in real life.

Fourth, we must seek to halt the trend to monopolistic and oligopolistic control. Over the last twenty years, the top one hundred companies have dramatically increased their share of the Community's total gross domestic product and it is a process which is obviously intensifying. It is likely that in Britain, for example, many small and medium-sized enterprises could be overwhelmed by that advancing merger tide. As usual, those who preach the sermons of competition most frequently and piously will be those who will be most assiduously involved in seeing that that very competition is reduced by takeover. A vigorous anti-trust policy is therefore needed to uphold the interests of consumers, workers, and smaller businesses and it patently has to be international in order to deal with the present and future realities of ownership and operation. Without that, the requirements of accountability to employees, to customers and to the communities of Europe, of protections and improvement of the environment, of health and safety regulation and of fair trading practices will not be met.

Fifth, we must seize the opportunity of these Euro-elections and the coming of the Single Market to make our concern for the environment a natural and inseparable part of our cause. As the environmental stresses and dangers become more obvious than ever and as the hazards of inadequately regulated industrial, agricultural and urban development become more complex, we have the need and the chance to be more assertive about our principled and practical view that people and the environment in which they live and on which they depend must take precedence over short term profit. It is not a regressive and eccentric conviction. On the contrary it is realism itself. Neither the interests of humanity nor of efficiency can be served by the pollution and exhaustion of our habitat. If socialism had never existed it would now have to be invented in order to ensure that there is a

6

consistent political commitment to democratic planning, to balanced development, to regulation of the inputs and outputs of production and to the other ingredients of conservation and improvement policies. Such policies for the environment will rarely be voluntarily, universally or thoroughly practised in an economic and social system run according to the preferences of the market. It is the 'people first' requirements of democratic socialism that must be implemented if the common interests of this and future generations in the Community are to prevail. Sixth, the concept of the 'social dimension' of the Community is one which must be widely and effectively applied. There will be strong resistance – especially from that area of the Right associated with the British Prime Minister – that is contemptuous of the whole idea that the development of the Single Market should be conditional in any way upon the significant strengthening of regional and social programmes. That resistance must be overcome, for the fact is that, as all experience teaches, a gap between economic development and social provision will inflict disadvantage on millions across the continent and cost and division on everyone else. We must vigorously assert, therefore, that the Social and Regional funds must be substantial enough to offer support to those parts of the Community which will most feel the disruptive effects of the new market arrangements, and be most likely to be denied the opportunity for advance if the market is left to develop as a commercial area that pulls wealth, production and employment incessantly to the centre.

Before and after 1992 we need to insist upon the commitment to balanced industrial and economic regeneration. If 1992 is focussed purely upon the free movement of goods, capital and labour, it will actually create the free movement of poverty, unemployment and depression. For that reason we have to offer instruments for balance that will include at least the following:

- The acceptance of the principle and practice of government or EC intervention for the purpose of ensuring development in

regions that do not have advantages of location in the central
area of the single market.
-   The means of maintaining industrial activity across the market.
-   The encouragement of productive and competitive industry
    by targeted investment and research and training.
-   The achievement of a European strategy for the development
    of science and technology.
-   The achievement of economies of scale by means other than
    monopolistic market domination.
-   Upward harmonization in rights and conditions at work,
    including decision-making structures in industry.
-   A genuine intra-EC trade policy that prevents one country
    from acquiring a massive surplus at the expense of another.

The adoption of this general approach will create a balanced
industrial policy that will include the following components:

-   Major investment in training and retraining (including language
    training) in the recognition that the skills of any industry's
    workforce are the most important asset in a rapidly changing
    and very competitive world.
-   Major investment in new technologies and research and development,
    which must be effectively co-ordinated at a European
    level.
-   Major investment in Europe's infrastructure, particularly telecommunications
    and transport, which is an essential component
    of balanced economic and industrial growth.
-   A common European approach to the transnational corporations,
    and to foreign investment in Europe. Such a common
    approach will of course be difficult to achieve, given the
    important regional interests that exist, but it is a necessary
    component of industrial development.
-   The establishment of Joint Sector Committees for each major
    industrial sector, which should include representatives of
    both sides of industry as well of the institutions of the EC.

Their main purpose will be the preparation of industrial development plans for each of the key sectors.
- Expansion of the Regional Fund to ensure a balanced spread of industrial development, and co-ordination of Regional Fund investment with the lending instruments for which borrowing is undertaken by the Commission, principally the European Investment Bank.
- Greater flexibility within the competition rules of the EC, to ensure that industrial development in the depressed parts of the Community is encouraged.

Of course, an important part of the success of such an industrial policy to strengthen the supply side of the European economy is the creation of a context of increasing demand, which is the reason the British Labour Party continues to assert the vital need for policies of co-ordinated European economic growth, including co-ordinated fiscal expansion. In such a co-ordinated process, the different problems that individual member countries face must be recognized and there must be clear rules of operation so that gains and sacrifices are fairly distributed.

As a result, we favour a policy of managed internal trade within the Community. We believe that movement of trade and resources must be managed formally and publicly or it will, in effect, be organized (especially at times of economic pressure) by private and informal means. By managed trade, I mean a strategy to ensure that expansion is not the source of uncontrollable deficit for any individual country.

Those countries that are willing to expand, and thus to create jobs at home and, consequently, in the rest of Europe, should be encouraged by the knowledge that their expansion will not collapse in financial crisis. To achieve this, we must first establish by agreement the maximum level of deficit which any one country may reasonably be expected to finance without provoking a crisis. Second, we must agree that any country which is running its maximum deficit, and so sustaining demand for the producers of others, will be allowed to use any means that do not discriminate between countries or industries to prevent that trade deficit from rising further. Any measures that do discriminate between countries, or between industries, should be seen as the protectionist measures that they are, and forbidden. If countries know they have powers, agreed with their trading partners, to prevent trade deficits from rising to crisis levels, then they can expand without fear, bringing benefits to themselves and to the rest of Europe.

It is the economic and industrial policies set out above which will form the basis of a modern economic future for Europe and secure the economic and social welfare of the people of our continent.

Of course, an important part of that strategy of balanced economic regeneration must be fundamental reform of the Common Agricultural Policy. A policy which, as Britain's National Consumer Council demonstrated recently after detailed research imposes support costs of up to £13.50 a week on every family in Britain, can be of no benefit to consumers. A policy which at the same time damages the small producers in the EEC and all food producers in the rest of the world must be changed. It must be an economic and social priority for all of us.

Operation of those instruments of balanced economic growth is vital, not to stifle enterprise or to tie growth down with red tape, but for the contrary purpose of promoting full development of potential and fair provision for people throughout the Community. They are requirements both of justice and of efficiency. The alternative to those directions is permanent imbalance and all of the cost, congestion, underperformance and resentments that will come in a centre-heavy Community.

The values which are central and common among the peoples of Western Europe with all their diversities are those of democracy, community, choice and freedom of decision, taste, thought and conduct under the law. But these values are only real if people are economically enfranchised by being materially secure. The need for a consistent and comprehensive Community strategy for balance in economic and social development, therefore, is at the core of any meaningful idea of a European *Community*

It is also very much a democratic socialist and European value that the qualities of life and liberty are too great, too precious to humanity to be confined to our national boundaries. The idea of *Community* must be projected to embrace the causes of peace, common security, development and freedom from racial, sexual, political and economic persecution across the world. These are essential to our idea of civilization. We know – in the words of the great British Socialist and internationalist Aneurin Bevan – that 'each freedom is only made secure by adding another to it'. This is the future facing Europe, and we must make it happen.

The European Community is more than a free-trade zone

Willy Claes
Deputy-Prime Minister and Minister of Economic Affairs and the Plan (Belgium)

INTRODUCTION

Since the beginning of the 1980s, the single internal market has been gaining in credibility. Economic studies carried out under the aegis of the Commission have shown that the potential advantages of the completion of the internal market, in both micro- and macro-economic terms, are considerable.

Moreover, the spectacular decisions of the European Council of Ministers, on such matters as the liberalization of the capital market, harmonization of standards relating to pollution and the mutual recognition of diplomas, testify to complete the various stages of the integration process on schedule. One of the best indications of this new-found credibility is the sudden interest and expressions of concern, appeals and warnings being issued by our international partners, whether it be the United States, Japan or the newly industrialized countries.

Within the Community itself, there is not a single merger, co-operation agreement, or even meeting of a professional body, from taxi drivers to press magnates, which does not make some reference to 1992. However, this potential new driving force may well turn out to be a damp squib or, even worse, develop into a blind and destructive struggle, if the 'invisible hand' of the

13

single market is not guided by a coherent set of policies reflecting specific options.

The greatest danger at present is that the Community might be reduced to a free-trade area within which rules, standards, taxation, currencies and social protection measures are determined by a Darwinian selection process resulting in a general falll in standards and an abandonment of the basis values on which the Treaty of Rome was drawn up. It is precisely those values which socialists more than anyone else, are concerned to defend. Socialism means doing more than just letting market forces operate; it means implementing regional, national and European policies which promote a sense of common purpose and reflect major decisions of strategy. Increased unification of the European market requires neither over-regulation nor unbridled deregulation, but a change in regulation promoting a competitive Europe based on a social and political consensus. While it would be naive now to defend a system of central planning of which Eastern Bloc countries have had such an unhappy experience, it would be just as unreasonable to entrust the future of our industrial society to irrational forces the perverse effects of which were exposed during recent economic and financial crises. The right approach is to combine greater freedom of supply and choice with concerted policies which complement and correct market forces.

In considering this problem a broad interpretation needs to be applied to industrial policy. Industrial policy means more than issuing a few directives on production. It also covers rules governing the behaviour of undertakings, the operation of markets and the social implications of economic events in terms of both vocational training and working conditions. Clear and credible framework policies in these fields are absolutely essential for the single market, but today these are sadly lacking. Over and above these measures, determined action in the form of a full-blown industrial policy should be an integral part of the European project.

CONCENTRATION AND THE GENERAL INTEREST

The economy is not an end in itself, but a means for implementing a certain conception of society. That conception of society should be reflected both at micro-economic level and in overall decisions. In this respect, the status of undertakings, their economic and financial operation and the relations between them are of prime importance for ensuring furtherance of the general interest.

Restructuring and concentration operations are currently on the increase. The acquisition of controlling shares and mergers in particular are allowing undertakings to free themselves from operations outside their main field of activity and to focus again on their chief area of interest. They can also facilitate exploitation of economies of scale, greater geographical coverage and a more advanced international division of labour within the European market. Since 1985, there has indeed been a greater increase in Community-type mergers and takeovers than in the international context outside the Community and in the purely national context even if the latter are still far more common. It must also be noted that such concentrations are mainly carried out by the largest undertakings in the Community, and not by small or medium-sized undertakings.

It must be emphasized also that in addition to the potentially favourable effects of concentrations, there is a whole series of consequences which may adversely affect the legitimate interests of certain parties – minority shareholders, creditors and especially workers and the general public, be it at regional, national or European level. As recent financial operations on which the fate of whole sectors of our economy depends have shown, there is a serious danger of international weakening of the control of large industrial and financial companies, with the lack of a clearly identified partner making it impossible to protect the interests of other parties. The transfer of decision-making centres is not acceptable unless it can be counterbalanced by matching political or trade union power.

15

Indeed, these restructuring and concentration operations often lead to risks being transformed to weaker third parties. Certain groups, for example, impose burdens of behaviour patterns on member companies who will thereby be exposed to increased risks, losses or reduced profits. This will inevitably affect their shareholders, creditors, workforce and even the local community. The right of bankruptcy can even be used as a technique for economic restructuring rather than a means of protecting the legitimate interests of the parties belonging to the undertaking concerned. What is more, in many cases the attempt to build up a controlling stake in a company is prompted by the desire for short-term financial gain through speculation and manipulation of information strategies rather than concern for more efficient production.

CONTROLLING MAJOR GROUPS BY A NEW BODY OF COMPANY LAW

Existing legislation in this field, both in Belgium and at Community level has so far proved unsatisfactory. Belgian legislation does not recognize groups of companies as such and provides for no special protection in relation to them. The general interest itself is largely devoid of protection against the behaviour of the group which nonetheless often has macro-economic repercussions or affects whole sectors. Courts are forced to have recourse to common law to protect shareholders and creditors who are victims of certain group activities. Similarly, as far as the workers are concerned judicial practice in the sphere of labour law endeavours to consider the group as a single undertaking particularly when it comes to industrial elections, the shutdown of undertaking and employment contracts: the definition of 'same employer', for example, is to be adapted to the particular characteristics of groups of undertakings. The fact remains that these efforts are limited and insufficient.

At European level too, fact precedes the law and the lack of a proper body of European company law, including regulation of transnational groups, will be increasingly felt particularly by

16

workers wishing to negotiate with an invisible manager. It is time that existing programmes in this field, particularly on the statute of the European public limited liability company, were implemented in order to guarantee the workforce of undertakings information and participation in the decision-making process at Community level. In this respect, the introduction in some large undertakings, of works councils and consultation on group strategy at transnational level is a step in the right direction. In the particular area of take-over bids present arrangements are also inadequate. Until now Belgium has stood out because of the absence of satisfactory regulations in this field, leaving too great a discretionary power to the Banking Committee, which is itself subject to many pressures. However, at a time when those building up conglomerates and launching dawn raids are concerned more with financial scheming than creating productive organizations and when the speculators may well get the upper hand over the entrepreneurs, a rigorous system of information and transparency must be demanded. In 1973 Belgium adopted clear regulations granting works councils more rights to information particularly in the case of a takeover bid, but there is not much sign that they are actually being enforced. Moreover, all the staff of a company which is subject to a takeover bid, whether friendly or hostile, should be informed of the strategic prospects of the operation regardless of who the controller is.

In July 1988 I introduced a bill on the publicizing of major shareholdings in listed companies and regulating takeover bids. The same problems have prompted similar concern in other industrialized countries. This is largely what led the Commission of the European Communities to submit to the Council of Ministers of the Communities a proposal for a directive on the publication of information on the buying and selling of major shareholdings in a listed company.

In a decentralized economy there is a need for strict provisions
on competition. It would be naive to think that the emergence of
major groups and the proliferation of mergers are due solely to
the desire for optimum adaptation to the market. In the case of
large undertakings they are often due to the desire to monopolize
the market. Such monopolization occurs at the expense of consumers who are forced to pay higher prices and put up with
abuses of dominant positions. Small and medium-sized undertakings are exploited by the company which has the monopoly
and workers risk losing their jobs as a result of production
cutbacks.

In Belgium every minister of Economic Affairs since 1975
has proposed improvements to the law of 27 May 1960 abolishing abuses of economic power, but in practice, this law still
contains a large number of shortcomings. To remedy this situation, I fully intend to submit a bill confirming the socialists'
resolve to fight these abuses.

At European level, the application of Article 86 of the
Treaty of Rome condemning these abuses of power has been
scarcely more effective, particularly as regards concentrations.
Article 86 only allows for control after the event, when the
merger or acquisition of holdings has already taken place. The
result is that if the operation is condemned by the Commission
and possibly by the European Court of Justice, the process must
in theory be annulled by dismantling the whole operation. Since
the cost is economic, financial and human terms of restoring the
original situation is generally prohibitive, it is very difficult to
implement this provision. Prior screening, however, at Community level, of the most important mergers would help to avoid
such costs. This is the aim of the new set of regulations proposed
by the Commission. If we really want to control the dangers of
monopolization of European markets by multinational companies then this proposal should be supported.

18

It is clear that some interventions at national level, particularly in the form of aid, may distort competition within the EEC. This is particularly true in countries where large undertakings dominate a particular sector and are actively supported by their public authorities. Many of these types of intervention do not achieve their aims and are a waste of resources, because, being adopted simultaneously in different European countries, they tend to cancel each other out or transfer the risks and difficulties from one state to another. In this situation, small countries are vulnerable to Europe's 'great powers' which are often better equipped to make their voice heard and to win acceptance for their opinions with the Community authorities. It must however be stressed that one of the main objectives of the Community is to maintain solidarity between its members, solidarity between regions, countries and between the 'North' and 'South'. The Single Act lays particular stress on such solidarity, and the considerable strengthening of the structural funds provides the resources to make it a reality. A view of Europe which took only the allocative function to the market into consideration and ignored its important distributive function as a token of EEC economic and social cohesion, would betray the very spirit of European integration. Consequently, I believe that, along with the condemnation of national aid which unilaterally distorts Community trade, there should be a willingness to implement common policies to enable countries and regions to overcome their structural handicaps, and develop joint strategies leading to better European competitiveness. This is precisely the aim of industrial policy as the Socialists see it.

INDUSTRIAL POLICY AND EUROPEAN COMPETITIVENESS

In all industrialized countries, the authorities use various schemes to encourage private industrial enterprise, to spread the effects of a decline, to restructure or liquidate certain activities, and finally to take over responsibility for certain large-scale

19

projects. The nature of the instruments used may be comprehensive and non-selective, as in the case of a change in the general taxation structure or may be restricted to certain industries, such as textiles, or to a particular undertaking. In Belgium, for example, a general set of policies has been used, including favourable tax arrangements for risk capital income, an exchange rate policy which aims to bring the Belgian franc into line with the strong currencies in order to limit the effects of rises in prices and costs and to maintain productivity, and a selective public investment policy. As for sector related policies, it is worth mentioning the economic expansion laws which help cope with structural difficulties of certain sectors and regions, the national and regional public economic initiative (regional investment companies), which has contributed to industrial redeployment through acquisition of holdings in existing undertakings and the creation of new undertakings and that of research and public procurement. It was with this in mind that I proposed in my 1975 communication to Parliament on 'a new industrial policy' a whole series of practical measures to promote technological research projects. Measures of this kind have been introduced in all European countries with varying degrees of success, and whether we like it or not they are here to stay. This brings up two types of question with respect to 1992. First at a time when deregulation is the prevailing fashion, is there any theoretical justification for the existence of industrial policies? And second, what are the prospects and advantages of a coherent and integrated European industrial policy?

SUPPLEMENTING MARKET FORCES

For those who have complete confidence in market forces, the existence of a healthy macro-economic climate is all that is really necessary and any industrial policy is redundant. The selective operation of the market and the spontaneous forces of competition are deemed sufficient to regulate the relationships between the various economic operators. Any form of targeted industrial policy on the other hand, is viewed negatively. According to this view, policies aimed at slowing down the process of structural change or sustaining sectors in decline ought to be rejected since the more the decline of an industry was prolonged the greater the damage would be to the rest of the economy. In any case there is no concrete evidence to suggest that prolonged adjustment is easier to bear than rapid rationalization. 'Positive' industrial policies which aim to speed up structural change are also condemned. Firstly, given the lack of suitable criteria, the government would not be capable of deciding which industries to promote, and secondly this type of interference would lead to a 'corporatist' system where economic decisions become politicised and freedom of initiative is stifled.

Need I say that this view is not shared by Socialists. The harmful effects of this type of laisser-faire policy have been obvious to us for a long time.

Moreover, our view is supported by much recent research which has questioned the effectiveness of the market's ability to make unassisted choices for new industrial structures. Having dismissed the notion, therefore, that industrial policy would be no more than a new name for protectionism, two arguments are worth stating. Firstly, there are the many shortcomings of the market, that is, situations in which market indicators alone, in particular prices, cannot be relied upon to make the best choices in the general interest. For example, new technological industries involving intensive research and economies of scale, lie outside the traditional model of competition and require public intervention. One well-known fact is that underinvestment in research and development, compared with the level that would be socially desirable, arises in cases where the results of research by one undertaking greatly benefit other undertakings which have not made the same investment. These 'external effects' are reflected in the difficulty experienced by private producers in benefitting from the results of their own efforts. This leads to them spending too little in these areas. In the same way, insufficient initiatives are taken in high-risk areas and areas for

21

which insurance systems are either incomplete or non-existent. One important aspect is the burden of the economic and social cost of adjustment and mobility in an economy which is in a persistent state of underemployment. More generally speaking, the existing price system is likely in a large number of cases to fail to emit the correct signals on the relative scarcity of resources, and moreover economic operators may well fail to react correctly to these signals even if they are correct. So the public authorities can usefully stimulate cooperation promoting the integration of the external effects of major technological decisions and promote competitiveness.

They should support, by means of financial aid and special public programmes, research and development in high technology industries (micro-computer, aerospace and biotechnological industries etc.) affected by high unrecoverable fixed costs; they should ensure a minimum socialisation of risk for activities where risk levels and incomplete information tend to curtail time-scales excessively, and reduce socially desirable levels of resource flows. Macro-economic regulation alone is not enough to deal with this type of problem and may even have perverse effects, for situations vary greatly from one industry to another, because of price inelasticity, insufficient demand or unemployment. Only a more detailed analysis of situations in different product of production factor markets would enable us to identify these causes and possibly to suggest appropriate solutions. Conversely, it is wrong to believe that the effects of comprehensive intervention on the allocation and distribution of resources are neutral. Macro-economic constraints and industrial behaviour are not necessarily compatible. Specific industrial policies which take into account the particular characteristics and interdependence of markets are what is required.

THE NEW STRATEGIC COMPETITION

A second argument in favour of industrial policy measures is the need to take a more realistic view of national and international trade. This has emerged from the research of both academics and management consultants. Over and above purely macro and micro-economic 'mechanisms', the authorities and private operators are today recognized as the 'agents' who, up to a certain point, are capable of changing the climate in which they operate to their own advantage. The functioning of national and international economies depends on strategic relationships through which firms and public authorities are materially or psychologically capable of creating advantageous situations for themselves and forcing the actions and reactions of existing and potential rivals. The aim will be to cooperate with one's competitors upstream whilst remaining keenly competitive as regards the actual final product; to erect credible barriers against operators liable to come onto the market; to control the range of products or services likely to supplant one's own activity; to modify one's bargaining power vis-à-vis suppliers and buyers and to influence the balane of power by making strategic moves and anticipating changes.

In this context, undertakings, states and regions are involved in a dynamic nexus of relationships, in which the implementation of new forms of organization, the opening up of new markets and the introduction of new products and production methods are constantly altering the balance and, changing the rules of the game in favour of some of the parties involved to the detriment of the others.

So how can we define the role of the public authorities, be they regional, national or European? They certainly cannot replace private operators because, despite their advantages (large financial resources, regulatory power, ability to work towards long-term goals etc.), they suffer from various handicaps compared with the former (difficulty in obtaining and using detailed information on markets or production techniques, slowness to react, lack of follow-up on problems, red tape, politicalization etc.). On the other hand, however, there is no empirical evidence or any general theoretical argument to suggest that the public authorities would be intrinsically incompetent whilst the private sector would automatically be more competent. The Belgian textile plan, thanks to which a crisis-hit industry has been successfully modernized, provides an example of harmonious cooperation between the public and private sectors.

Conversely the case of the Belgian steel industry has shown how the private sector can hand over responsibility to the community for a sector in difficulty which it had been incapable of modernizing in time, thus avoiding contributing financially towards saving and restructuring it.

With a view to the new strategic competition, the idea behind the proposed public initiative is not that it should be limited to macro-economic regulation alone, nor implement rigid industrial planning nor manage sectors in decline, but provide a varied strategic framework in which to promote industrial dynamism. International competition is not as it appears in political economy handbooks: rather it is a subtle game where the parties involved are placed asymmetrically in relation to one another and where in some cases political considerations exert an influence which is likely to tip the balance in favour of one particular company, region, nation or group of nations. As recent examples show, transfers of technology, international credit conventions, the requirements for setting up a company abroad or obtaining an important supply contract, depend on power relationships and alliances which are capable of substantially restricting or enlarging the scope of industrial strategies.

This is something which has been grasped by some public figures who are endeavouring to promote industrial revival.

In the aerospace industry, the electronics industry, the agro-industry, the bio-industry, they have a role to play in restoring the balance of relations between the domestic undertakings of a region, large multinationals, and the other public authorities. They are able in particular, to provide information on alternative partners, to make strategic use of public procurement policy and negotiate inter-state agreements with third countries (mainly developing countries) who are more willing to negotiate with states than with companies.

24

THE DEVELOPMENT OF EUROPEAN-WIDE STRATEGIES

This brings me to a second question, the importance of the European dimension. The Community clearly enjoys a number of advantages when it comes to the implementation of a credible industrial strategy – its strong position in world trade negotiations, its capacity for industrial restructuring and division of labour on a continental scale, close interdependence between member countries contrasted by little interdependence between the EEC and the rest of the world, vast resources for social reorganization and transnational cooperation capable of making Europe lead the world.

But it is only during the last few years that European strategies have begun to emerge. Whilst the Treaty of Rome contained explicit provisions on common agricultural, economic, competition, employment, trade, transport and tax harmonization policies, it contains not the slightest reference to industrial policy. The ECSC and EURATOM treaties on the other hand, without quoting the exact term, expressed the resolve to implement an industrial policy for coal, steel and atomic energy. The first explicit analysis of this topic by the European authorities is contained in the memorandum addressed by the Commission to the Council in 1970 and entitled 'the Community's industrial policy'. According to its authors, 'founded 12 years ago, the Community has just emerged from its transition period, during which a common market in merchandise was brought to completion. It now enters on a new phase of progress. A common industrial development policy encouraging the creation of a European industrial 'fabric' is indispensable if three vital objectives are to be achieved: the establishment of firm foundations for the economic – and soon the political – unity of Europe, the maintenance of economic growth, and a reasonable degree of technological independence of major world powers.' The main aims of industrial development were and still are the following:
- Better working conditions and proper appreciation of services particularly for those doing manual work to prevent the

workers turning their backs on industry.
- More active participation by workers in the selection of development targets and in the operation of firms.
- Harmonization of education to promote the free movement and freedom of establishment of executive staff and consequently economic and industrial unification.
- Protection of the natural environment to give direction to industrial development taking more account of the responsibilities incurred by local authorities as a result of industrial mergers.
- More harmonious distribution of the world's wealth, given that the Community can only benefit from an increase in the number of prosperous trading partners, but must be ready to accept the progressive and orderly transfer of certain industrial activities to the developing countries.

In spite of its good points, the memorandum is unsatisfactory. There is a marked contrast between the wealth of information and thought it contained on the Community industrial situation and the imprecion of the policy guidelines proposed. However, despite its lack of clear political commitment, it took until the Paris Declaration of October 1972 for governments to express their support for this industrial and technological policy. The declaration, which was prepared by the permanent representatives with the help of a group of senior officials, stated in particular that: 'the Heads of State and Government feel there is a need to try and provide uniform foundation for industry throughout the Community. This entails the removal of technical barriers to trade and elimination, especially in the field of taxation and law, of obstacles hindering alignment and concentration amongst undertakings, swift adoption of a statute for the European company, the progressive and effective opening up of public contracts, the promotion on European scale of competitive undertakings in advanced technology, the adaption and redevelopment, under socially acceptable conditions of industrial branches in difficulty, the preparation of provisions to guarantee that concentrations, affecting undertakings established in the Community, are compatible with the Community's socio-economic goals, and fair competition under the treaty provisions both within the common market and on the outside markets... Objectives should be defined and the development of a common scientific and technological policy ensured'. We have had to wait 15 years for this declaration to begin to be implemented. There has been considerable progress in abolishing non-tariff trade barriers and in the implementation of common technology programmes, ESPRIT, BRITE, RACE and even EUREKA. The impetus, albeit partly artificial, given by the prospect of 1992 has sped up the adoption of new directives. By early 1988, the Commission had proposed 211 of the 300 directives or regulations set out in the White Paper. These include such progressive steps consolidating the European industrial area as preference for European standards as opposed to other specifications, the creation of a common transport market, consumer protection in respect of price labelling and the gradual liberalization of banking and insurance services.

SOME PRACTICAL MEASURES TO PROMOTE SOLIDARITY BASED ON A PROJECT FOR SOCIETY

However the future after 1992 is still uncertain. If the authorities responsible considered the completion of the internal market as an end in itself, they would fall well short of our expectations.

The creation of a single market and the corresponding growth in interdependence create both the opportunity and the need for additional measures to exploit the Community dimension strategically and severally.

In specific terms, we have at our disposal today a wide range of public initiatives which are compatible with a decentralized European economy and would involve:

– Subsidizing research into new methods of production.

- Taking responsibility for part of the risk involved in innovatory strategy.
- Promoting the transfer of university research findings to the fields of production and marketing.
- Removing obstacles to the spread of new technology among traditional industries.
- Contributing to the setting up, reorganization of expansion of private companies.
- Helping SMUs by reducing their overheads (simplifying administration and providing special export aid) and improving their access to information (data banks, computer networks etc.).
- Promoting co-operation in research, industry – university – public sector.
- Organizing the retraining of workers affected by restructuring and training public and private managers to cope more effectively with the complex tasks of management and strategy.
- Giving workers a right to in-service training.

These initiatives and policies should be coordinated, both within the Community area and in relation to the rest of the world so as to avoid discrimination, uncontrolled external repercussions and costly overlapping. Be it for expanding sectors or industries in decline, a concerted approach allows for better distribution of adjustment costs, the widespread application of the results achieved and the efficient implementation of common policies. This approach should also prevent 'social Europe' from falling behind 'economic Europe' and create the conditions for a consensus between the two sides of industry in the Community. The formation of such a European consensus should be an integral part of an industrial policy. Without a social dialogue involving governments, administrations, representatives from the workers and managers of undertakings on the overall aims of the European industrial society and the principal methods to be implemented, there is a risk that the 1992 challenge will result in disorder. But given differences of national sensitivity such a consensus will be by no means easy to achieve. Meanwhile the role of national strategies is crucial. Were they to be dismantled before the implementation of Community strategies, economic and social operators would be placed in a dangerous institutional vacuum. The fact remains that national systems will gradually give way to a European or even worldwide perspective, especially in the case of small, open economies like those of the Benelux countries. The regional dimension will continue to be relevant in Europe, however, in so far as it permits practical action geared to real problems and local resources. As pointed out in the Padoa-Schioppa report the correct level of government is the lowest level at which the function in question can be effectively carried out. It is only if a substantial proportion of the costs and advantages go beyond the chosen level that there is a risk of the action being partially ineffective. In creating flexibility as regards the effective competence of different levels of government, the Europe of 1992 will have to be careful to maintain coordination and transfers between these different levels in order to safeguard the essential links of solidarity between them.

In conclusion it is not so much a time for deregulation as for a change of regulation. The role of a Community industrial policy is more necessary than ever in this change. It is one of the main vehicles through which Europe will gradually forge its identity and autonomy in relation to the other great industrial powers. It is also one of the channels through which the resolve to integrate economic and social considerations must find expression in a model for society.

Such a policy should not be the product of over-cautious protectionism or of central planning, but be based on strategic decisions arising from a political consensus.

Europe: a new frontier for social democracy?

Jacques Delors
President of the European Commission

From the very beginning, at the turn of the century, social democracy was hotly debated within the socialist movement. Tried and tested by power and events, after World War I and more especially after World War II, the social democratic model triumphed in Europe. During the 1970s it served as a benchmark, even in countries whose past had robbed them of the basic conditions for social democracy.

It must be said that the social democratic model proved its economic and social worth. Indeed, the sheer diversity of its visible embodiments in countries with traditions and cultures as different as Federal Germany, the Scandinavian countries, Austria and the United Kingdom suggested that it could be used anywhere in the world.

Then, at the end of the 1970s, the scene suddenly changed. All it took was a tax rebellion for social democracy to suffer political reverses. People tend to forget that, quintessentially democratic, social democracy can admit of electoral defeat and there was talk of malaise, of running out of steam, of crisis. But crises are in fashion, because our fretful, disillusioned societies consume ideas as they consume material goods.

But in this mindless whirl, in which anything goes, a few great movements do know where they are going and European integreation is one of them. What if Europe were to be the theatre in which social democracy accomplishes its mission? What if Europe were to provide the means? What if the European dimension were to prove inevitable in the face of all the internal or external changes that have outdated the social democratic model?

That is what I would like to suggest, but first let me review the basic tenets of social democracy.

THE FOUNDATIONS OF THE SOCIAL DEMOCRATIC MODEL

The social democratic enterprise today is faced with two challenges which singly and in combination are threatening its progress: the external challenge of globalization and the internal challenge presented by new aspirations and attitudes. From within and from without the principles and the institutions from which social democracy in Europe draws its strength are under attack.

To grasp this fully, we must, however briefly, return to the fountainhead. From its inception, social democracy linked emancipation of the working classes with the broader aim of a democratic society. This reformist view, which broke with the socialist tradition of the early days of the industrial revolution, set it in stark opposition to the revolutionary approach. To Lenin, who complained that its myopic gradualism stood surety for the chimera of bourgeois democracy, Kautsky retorted, with a certain grandeur, that the irruption of the labour movement into politics had changed the nature of the political debate and hence the nature of democracy. That far-reaching debate was to leave an enduring mark on Europeans. Indeed, it is still visible today for anyone who is alert to new signs emanating from the east.

However, it is not that debate but rather the internal consistency binding the principles of social democracy, its methods and instruments, that merit our attention today.

32

The theoretical connection between the labour movement and democratic society was matched by a functional coupling between the trade union movement and the political party. It provided a permanent link between the social and political spheres, so that progress in one could not serve as an excuse for inaction in the other.

This combined movement was sustained, as I see it, by a dual compromise: firstly between capital and labour, and secondly between operation of the market and state intervention, which compensated for the market's deficiencies and curbed its excesses.

The legitimacy and effectiveness of the dual compromise were the focus of debate within the social democratic movement at the end of the 1970s. But perhaps no one could foresee at the time how far, through this very compromise, social democracy had transformed the nature of the State. The role of the State was to provide the framework for the dual compromise: in the one case, by its neutrality, acting as guarantor for the social debate; in the other, playing a full economic role, dedicated in particular to the production of public goods and guiding the future.

With this support, the dual compromise became enshrined in institutions and policies so effective that they have on occasion been mistaken for social democracy itself. Yet they drew their strength not from narrow pragmatism but from an ideology most often associated with Keynes and Beveridge:

- Keynesian policies were to go far beyond a cyclical management of overall demand; they ushered in a welfare state with broad regulation and distribution functions, as a back-up to the allocation function which was left entirely to the market.
- The organization of welfare inspired by Beveridge did much more than protect the material interests of wage earners; its integrating design extended solidarity to society as a whole.

Social democracy thus made an implicit contract with 'growth' and 'economic dynamism'. On the one hand, it set out to provide the conditions for growth and distribution of the benefits of growth. On the other hand, it fed on growth, particularly the growth of employment, since more employment was an increasingly decisive factor in financing social protection.

INTERNAL AND EXTERNAL CHALLENGES TO SOCIAL DEMOCRACY

The first test for social democracy came with the challenge of the successive oil shocks, followed by the slackening of international trade that coincided with a worldwide technological and industrial revolution. It struck at the mainspring of growth and employment, challenging the pertinence of Keynesian policies and the development of social protection, despite continual adjustments that strained relations between the party and the unions. Nevertheless, the quality of these relations enabled social democrats to turn in more than creditable relative performances. But then came another cause for alarm; more serious in that it came from within. The State, the other pillar of social democratic societies, was now weakened in its social, as well as its economic, foundations. The targets of social aspirations were in fact shifting onto ground where the State had little or no foothold: the new importance of local solidarity; the emergence of regional powers, better able to organize the synergy of economic, social and cultural forces in a complex universe; growing marginalization on the fringes of the welfare institutions; the march of social forces, which carried the struggle outside the traditional framework of arbitration, all highlighted the shortcomings of the State.

It may be an oversimplification, but post-war social democracy can be said to have linked success, and in some ways its destiny, to the full use of human resources and the regulatory function ultimately assumed by the State. This raises the question of whether social democracy is being overtaken by new advances in ideas and action. Our aim will simply be to show how European integration can facilitate this process and help social democrats meet the internal and external challenges now facing them.

Jacques Delors

The revitalization of European integration has been proceeding silently but strongly for the last five years. Since the 1984 Fontainebleau European Council, which put an end to family feuds and laid the foundations for renewal, a movement has taken shape. It encompasses far more than the unification of the domestic markets of the Twelve, to which some would like to reduce it, out of conviction or for strategic reasons. In fact it pursues the historic purpose of European political union enshrined in the new Community charter, the Single European Act. That Act demonstrates the Twelve's resolve to live the present and build the future together. This resolve takes the form of a dual affirmation:

- From now on, the Community's external identity (foreign policy coordination) and European economic integration (fulfilment of the Treaty of Rome) must go hand in hand.
- Economic integration will not be achieved merely through the interplay of market forces, unleashed by the removal of frontiers and the harmonization of rules. It will work only if sustained by a broader ambition, given material shape by operational common policies. What needs to be done now, on the basis of the Single European Act, is to recognize the specificity of social relations in Europe, to reduce inequalities and structural disparities between towns and regions, to combine research programmes and to take full account of the common heritage represented by the environment and the rural fabric.

These are no idle statements. The decisions taken first in Brussels, then in Hanover, in 1988 by the twelve Heads of State on reform of the instruments available to the Community have far-reaching financial implications. The credibility of the single European market has been strengthened by this, to the point that the European venture is now a fact of life for the future of the world economy.

Viewed as a whole, the European venture gives social democracy an opportunity to advance: enabling it to develop its international vocation, helping it to complete its historic tasks, making it receptive to new expectations in our societies.

INTERNATIONAL VOCATION

Staunch supporters of a more open economic system, with a global approach, notably to the Third World, social democrats have frequently been obliged to retreat to their national bases, if only because they had to be won back.

Yet at the same time liberal political forces have unself-consciously espoused the internationalization of markets, re-establishing links with the world mission of capitalism, which had been blurred by conservative nationalism. Responsibility for managing world affairs has thus shifted to the right of the political spectrum. An odd reversal, ill-disguised by an over-general and hence over-generous proclamation of the need for a new world order.

The Europe of 1992 could be an active instrument in introducing a new economic world order, if that were the common purpose of the Twelve. The international monetary and financial problems which are so bedevilling the economies of the poorer and weaker countries today might be summed up in a simple sentence: there is no pilot in the cockpit of what has become an increasingly interdependent world economy; market integration is not being matched by an international monetary regulation and financial redistribution capacity.

So far the Twelve have radically overhauled the machinery of the common agricultural policy and laid the foundations of an attractive and powerful European financial area. They now need to strengthen the European Monetary System so as to synchronize monetary and economic co-operation with the progress of financial integration.

If they succeed, the Twelve could have a decisive influence on the world economic order, indebtedness and monetary stability in four years' time. But would they want to use this influence? And to what purpose? The social democratic movement cannot

36

afford to ignore these questions which have ceased to be rhetorical since the Hanover European Council in June 1988.

A Europe which had regained an economic status commensurate with its demographic potential and its know-how would carry more weight in world affairs. It would also be in better position to deal with its own problems, beginning with unemployment.

None of Europe's economies is robust or resilient enough to break the stranglehold of international competition that is sharpening with interdependence: Japan today, south-east Asia tomorrow, other major newly-industrialized countries such as India, Brazil, Algeria, Turkey and Nigeria the day after. We all know the the answer is to aim high, to diversify into quality products and services and to introduce a radical reorganization of working time.

Meanwhile, low growth rates are sapping efforts to put public finances on a sound footing. Even Federal Germany, which was one of the first to embark on the saving cycle, is now faced with a Federal deficit that exceeds the limits allowed under the Basic Law. Similarly, social financing has lost all flexibility, at a time when a wave of new pensioners and longer life expectancy are adding to the benefits bill. A special restructuring effort will be needed to cope with the most pressing routine expenditure and step up spending in other areas: improving the quality of education; integrating the long-term unemployed. But without a new margin for manoeuvre, restructuring along these lines seems unattainable.

One of the efforts of European integration today is precisely to create new margins not only for growth but also for public finances and employment. This emerges quite clearly from an analysis of the specifically economic effects of implementing the Single European Act over the next few years. Its impact has been quantified in two ways depending on whether we are considering supply-side policies (the large market in the strict sense) or demand-side policies (the macro-economic accompaniment to the single European market):

- The improvement in European performance, brought about by the effects of scale, will create new margins for manoeuvre. Improved tax revenue and cheaper public procurement will reduce the burden on the public finances of each Member State by an average amount equivalent to 2.2 points of GDP in the medium term. This gain is comparable with the overall improvement recorded between 1981 and 1988.
- Exploitation of this margin for manoeuvre, as part of a concerted budget and taxation policy strategy, would have an appreciable effect on both growth and employment. Admittedly, it would not be enough to bring unemployment down to the low-water mark reached just before the first oil shock, but it should be enough to reverse the trend by creating an additional 4 million jobs in the medium term.

It would of course be for each Member State to decide, in the light of its own priorities and constraints, what use to make of these new possibilities. In other words, the European approach does not seek to erode the powers of national authorities but rather to restore a margin of autonomy which will enable them to perform their essential tasks. Globalization plus regionalization does not, as some extremists have suggested, leave social democracy with no alternative but to yield to the State. The European approach would enable a reformed State to resume its function of providing consistency and guidance. And because social democracy is at heart essentially concerned with access to employment and management of the labour market, it would not be long before it discovered the secrets of a new link between three tiers of responsibility:

- the Community tier, where the capacity for macro-economic action operates most efficiently in favour of overall growth and employment;
- the national tier, where the budgetary, fiscal and parafiscal incentives most likely to transform labour market structures can be identified (intensity of recourse to capital and labour;

configuration of skills, qualifications and experience; renewal of company networks);
- the regional tier, where vacancies and job applications can be matched, the unemployed can be integrated and research, financing and production functions can complement each other.

A SUPPORT FOR NEW TASKS

With its momentum impeded by external constraints, social democracy is also seeing its basic principles contested. This is the internal challenge it faces, reflecting a threefold trend:
- relationships in production have changed with the new industrial revolution;
- the working class is gradually blending with a vaguely-defined middle class, leaving poor and marginalized groups who do not benefit from this mobility;
- democracy, constantly sought after but never achieved, is today threatened by new forms of domination.

The question raised by these changes could be summed up as follows: 'How can we live as social democrats in a post-industrial, post-working class society?'

I do not propose to go into this issue in depth. It is, nevertheless, the common thread of our joint enquiry. I would simply like to elucidate the type of mediation that the Community might offer to revive social democracy. Such mediation will actually assume its full meaning when it comes to forecast new relationships in production, meeting certain urgent collective needs or providing a response to current forms of manipulation and oppression.

NETWORKS, GROWTH POLES, COOPERATION: A NEW MIXED ECONOMY

Fierce rivalry between firms – aided and abetted by governments – on world markets and the trend towards economic concentration which seeks to sidestep it, have come to monopolize our thinking about competition.

However, the rise of the new technologies, and the redistribution of the productive functions in its wake, is accompanied by less obvious changes which could be attributed to the proliferation of cooperation between economic units, linked together by the service economy.

Thus we have company networks and development clusters in which firms cooperate closely without losing any of their autonomy. As part of the same trend, group configuration is moving towards greater decentralization and 'multidivisional' structures. To concentrate on strategic functions, large companies are 'farming out' less essential functions, which are making fortunes for small firms forming other complementary networks.

Economic geography is changing too. It is re-emphasizing the importance of local growth poles around an urban centre, whose motive force depends upon the density of interaction between universities, finance houses, labour market management services and local businesses. A new co-operation economy, a pendant to world competition, is developing around us. It can no longer be described in terms of input and output in a given area, but in terms of interacting networks and development poles.

The main features of the mixed economy introduced by social democracy are changing: the local dimension is again becoming more and more important and the nature of public intervention is altering as direct subsidies or the financing of productive investment give way to indirect incentives to co-operation.

The European area, offering as it does a continuity of cultures, a rich fabric of more than 2000 university centres with complementary specializations, and a dense communications network, is a natural breeding ground for this new mixed economy, in which competitive and cooperative forces are developing side by side.

It is therefore no accident that the European agenda is giving priority in 1988 and 1989 to strengthening competition and the social dimension of the single European market; that moves towards liberalization are being matched by steps to counter social dumping, by the implementation of new forms of research cooperation, by the definition of regional and rural development of conversion programmes.

Finding – or rather feeling our way towards – the optimum balance of responsibilities between Community, national and local authorities – will be one of our hardest tasks over the next few years. But upon it will depend the success of a new social democratic compromise between the State and the market.

DEALING WITH NEW COLLECTIVE PRIORITIES

Social democrats were among the first to introduce collective safeguards against the basic social risks. And if cracks are showing in the system today, they in no way invalidate the principle of solidarity; they simply suggest other ways of giving it expression. The same principle will have to be applied in dealing with new collective priorities. Preservation of the natural environment and the balance between town and country stand out conspicuously as operations to be mounted at European level. But there are certainly others.

Alarm, not to say anger, at the degradation of our natural heritage is no longer the prerogative of marginal groups or groups regarded as such. Nor is it confined to northerners. The Chernobyl disaster in 1987 served to highlight our shared vulnerability. We now know that major ecologic hazards are no respecters of frontiers.

Chronic pollution of North Sea coasts and fishing grounds, desecrated seabeds in the Mediterranean, inland waterways and groundwater saturated with nitrogenous fertilizers, mysterious mass disappearances of entire species of trees, are so many visible signs of impending disaster, so many warnings to a developing world that does not value nature.

41

Faced with this situation, Community countries could not do better than offer each other a helping hand. The framework and the means for large-scale action are provided by the Single European Act. It enables us:
- to agree on safeguards that will obviate distortions of competition;
- to set up joint agencies for mounting major operations, as on the Rhine or in the Mediterranean, where the task calls for coordination between several countries;
- to allocate common resources to the fight against pollution in the poorer regions, often the hardest hit.

Admittedly, national views differ on this as on many other issues. But what has been achieved so far is meagre, not to say disappointing.

What is needed is a fresh political inspiration if we are to cope with the sweeping changes that will come between now and the year 2000 as technological advances are applied to agriculture. The potential productivity of European agriculture, in the north and south alike, is enormous and in part stimulated by the reduction in price support. The development of irrigation and methods of biological control and stimulation would make it possible to release almost 6 million hectares (of a total of 25 million hectares) by the year 2000 while keeping output constant. Must we therefore resign ourselves to another massive flight from the land, to a new wave of urban concentration and desertification? Other courses are open to us which would preserve the age-old balance between town and country, the hallmark of European societies. Technical arrangements have been devised and proposed in the context of reform of the common agricultural policy: income subsidies, set-aside, extensification, rural development programmes. No doubt these arrangements can be improved upon but the main thing is our willingness to work together to improve planning.

COMBATING NEW FORMS OF ALIENATION AND INTOLERANCE

For social democrats, democracy means more than economic efficiency through social peace. Democracy is the involvement of everyone without exception in the building of society and hence the repudiation of re-emerging forms of alienation and intolerance. The European dimension gives new pertinance and prominence to issues which defy solution at national level.

Two topical examples are worth more than volumes of theorizing. The first example relates to what might be termed audiovisual alienation. Throughout the Community, audiovisual production, and its independence of the powers that be, have become a major issue for democracy. Because Europeans, and young Europeans in particular, are spending more and more of their free time in front of a television screen. Because privatization, the symbol of independence, is far from synonymous with creativity or pluralism. Do we have to accept that the pre-eminence of violence, sex and money on our screens is part of our freedom?

If audiovisual production is to acquire the civilizing dimension anticipated by Marshall McLuhan, the first prerequisite is that it should exist. Without the benefits of scale, European audiovisual production is being steadily supplanted by American and Japanese wares. Rediscovering a national or regional cultural dimension, in the age of satellite and cable, depends on a strong European audiovisual policy, covering technological standards as well as commercial rules.

A second example is the support that an on-going strategy of resistance to intolerance and racism could draw from the European framework. Dramatically so in France – but in Federal Germany, the United Kingdom, Belgium and the Netherlands too – racial intolerance has multiple roots, including of course the problems posed by the assimilation of existing migrants. The fact remains that this disquieting upsurge of intolerance coincides with an increase in the demographic imbalance between the two shores of the Mediterranean, an imbalance that cannot be corrected simply by means of traditional bilateral agreements.

The Twelve will obviously have to devise assimilation policies to dampen resentment and restore confidence in the future. Implementation of such policies presupposes the introduction of controls on new waves of migration, which in turn will call for active cooperation at European level. But assimilation and controls will not be enough. Within the next ten years the Community will have to lay the foundations for more practical cooperation with its Mediterranean partners, who may well have come together in a greater Maghreb.

United, Europeans could make a significant contribution to the growth these countries need if they are to welcome coming generations. This is surely a long-term political challenge, consonant with the repudiation of intolerance, which could be met by Europe's social democrats.

It is true that in a certain sense the social democratic model has become outdated, as Jean Monnet spoke of ideas being outdated when they are subsumed into a living reality. But social democracy is more than an idea. It is an inexhaustible source of political and social dynamism, because it is essentially based on respect for the individual as a free being in a social context.

Faced with new international challenges, the emergence of local aspirations and powers, and the weakening of national States, some believe that the time has come to base the social democratic ideal on the withering of the State. They hope that by basing themselves solely on human rights they can build a rampart against new forms of alienation. I cannot accept this, because it means yielding too quickly to passing fancies and abandoning political enterprise.

Far from dissolving the national States, the European dimension can give them meaningful scope for action once again. The European dimension does not resolve our problems, but it does offer an opening. It is for social democracy to seize this golden political opportunity!

A left programme for the European Community

Laurent Fabius
President of the National Assembly (France)

The forthcoming prospect of a large internal market raises a number of questions which the European Left will have to resolve without renouncing its principles.

Let us look first at its means of action. The message of the Left is, basically, internationalist. Until now most left-wing parties – whether Socialists or Social Democrats – have mainly used or proposed to use purely national instruments: separate systems of rules, national fiscal policy, industrial strategy relating to their own country, etc. The Single Market, once it has been completed, will automatically reduce the margin of autonomy of these national instruments. It will force the Left, whether in opposition or in power, to consider its actions in genuinely European terms. It is a challenge.

There is another challenge, relating not to the instruments of action but to its objectives. The Single Market is just one of the aspects of European integration. It must not only be a single market for products and capital; it must be a single area for the people, for exchanges between people, their ambitions and their hopes. It must represent not just a single market but also a common approach to scientific research, the environment, education, the audiovisual sector, defence policy, and so forth. The major objectives must become common objectives. The Left is not in power everywhere in Europe; far from it. And the Left has different approaches, on defence policy for example. So the parties of the Left must make a major and common effort to bring about a rapprochement between their views and gain the allegiance of the people. That is one of the most difficult tasks facing them in the coming years. It implies closer links than exist today between the various parties of the European Left.

The development of the Left, interlinked with that of Europe, will certainly give rise to some questioning of accepted views. At the same time it could prove fertile terrain for the forces of the Left in making us question some of our traditional approaches: the role of the public sector, the effectiveness of policies of social redistribution, educational methods, etc. It could also prove fertile ground for Europe itself, which will not really be completed unless it chooses the progressive option. If Europe bows only to the laws of the market it will become no more than a free-trade zone exposed to the greed of our major competitors. The people of Europe would not get anything out of it. Nor would the other countries of the world for it is only a strong Europe, one that is influential, cohesive and generous, that can make any real contribution to peace and development in the world. The basic idea is probably that of community. That implies equality, fraternity, liberty, the extension of democracy to all areas (political, social, economic and cultural). The idea of 'community' is like a hyphen between Europe and the Left. It is the target of both. Europe as a community needs Europe. The Left as a community needs Europe. That is one of the great challenges of the times to come.

Not all the Socialist, Labour or Social Democratic parties of Europe share the same terms of reference or the same history. But they do share the same ambition: economic efficiency accompanied by social justice. The economic aspect underpins the social one because there can be no redistribution without growth nor growth without competitiveness. But the social aspect also underpins the economic one because there can be no competitiveness without cohesion and no cohesion without justice. The

Left rejects the brutality of the liberal model as it does the impotence of the economic planning model.

Immediately after the second world war, the Left proposed an original strategy to the European nations, aimed at correcting economic and social imbalances while respecting the rights of the individual and the freedom of the enterprise. This gave rise to a specific way of life, distinct from American individualism or Japanese asceticism. Its main characteristics are well-known: rise in purchasing power, wider social protection, longer holidays, more democratic training, the introduction of civic rights in undertakings.

Today we must continue along that road within a changing environment. The market is changing: the increasing economic openness towards the outside, the technological revolution of the past ten years, the emergence of new industrial powers, especially in Asia, and the international monetary disturbances have imposed serious constraints on Europe and led to a radical restructuring, together with mass unemployment. Unemployment insurance expenditure, for instance, is rocketing, but the number of people excluded from it is increasing.

The large market wanted by the Member States of the European Community will accentuate this trend: it will sharpen the competition between undertakings and reduce the states' margin of manoeuvre in terms of both economic policy and structural intervention.

Can the Left propose a project for Europe that will reconcile the freedom of the undertaking with the equality of the people? Given that it does not worship either the market or the State, it is well placed to give an original answer. If dynamic undertakings are matched by dynamic government, the completion of Europe will lead to more growth, more employment and more justice. It is indeed up to the public authorities to lay down the rules of the competition game.

So the Left must follow two courses of action. It must avoid the main risks to the completion of the internal market: lack of coordination between national strategies which could lead to the development of policies of recession; blind deregulation, which would lead to excessive competition; a brutal form of restructuring, which would destroy the industrial fabric; the accentuation of inequalities between regions and between people, which would tear apart the social fabric. It must act at European level to renew the balance between market dynamism and appropriately adjusted government intervention, which led to the success of the recent years of construction and can do the same, following new procedures, for the years of modernization.

In more concrete terms, this project of the European Left must be based on four major, indissolubly linked policies: a policy of sustained growth with respect for the environment, a policy of fair competition, a policy of balanced industrial development and a policy of social progress.

A. SUSTAINED GROWTH WITH RESPECT FOR THE ENVIRONMENT

To begin with, the opening up to public contracts, the abolition of frontiers, the liberalization of financial services and the economies of scale following the completion of the common market will encourage greater productivity and a fall in production costs. Given the constraints of sharper competition between undertakings, these improvements should lead to a fall in prices. Europe can expect to see stronger growth and little inflation, thanks mainly to the revival of productive investment. According to surveys by 300 European experts under Mr Paolo Cecchini, the medium-term positive global impact of the large market will be in the region of 4.5 per cent to 7 per cent of GNP with the net creation of two to five million jobs.

Yet we will only see these positive effects if concerted flanking measures are taken. For the intensification of trade within the Community and the increase in non-Community imports if growth should speed up could in fact worsen the trade balance of countries whose balance is already fragile. If the states concerned react in an independent fashion, there is a strong risk

48

of recessionist policies developing, which would cause the Single Act to lose some of its momentum.

To forestall this danger – and that is a second point – the convergence of national policies must relate as much to trade policy as to monetary policy or measures to sustain growth.

The EEC is not a fortress of trade. Imports account for 10 per cent of its GNP, as against 6 per cent in Japan and 9 per cent in the United States, and the Community's customs tariff is among the lowest in the world. And after all, that is only natural: the Community could not be both the artisan of free trade in Community relations and a partisan of protectionism vis-à-vis third countries. But free trade does imply reciprocity: if the Community opens up to the outside world, the outside world must also open up to it. The unilateral abolition of non-tariff barriers would encourage deindustrialization and cancel out the positive effects of the large internal market. So the Left must work at building up a European commercial strategy based on a Community system to protect a small number of sensitive sectors (textiles, cars, electronic goods for the general public, etc.) which are currently subject to national measures of protection, and at obtaining counterparts for the Community's greater openness, whether on a bilateral or a multilateral basis. More generally, the Commission needs greater negotiating powers so that Europe can speak with one voice in the forums for trade talks and stand on an equal footing with its trade partners.

The convergence of national monetary policies is necessary in order to ensure that trade imbalances or the liberalization of capital flows are not reflected by fluctuations in exchange rates. This mechanism has become well known by now: the dollar falls, the Deutschmark goes up, the other European currencies are devalued and the national monetary authorities raise interest rates in an attempt to limit the disparities. By making borrowing more expensive, the increase in interest rates penalizes investment, and therefore employment. And above all, the disparities between interest rates distort the play of competition between European nations. If the chief results of the liberalization of capital movements were to accentuate monetary instability and increase the disparities between interest rates, it would obviously not be attaining the desired objective. So the economic and commercial aspect of Europe must go hand in hand with the monetary Europe: the large single market needs a common currency, with control over its issue and management.

A concerted policy to sustain growth is equally necessary. The main initiative must come from those European countries which have surplus savings. Today the fight against unemployment is the major objective of European integration. In the short term, the completion of the internal market may, however, be accompanied by job losses following the rise in productivity. When the internal market is completed it is, therefore, essential that we pursue a European policy to sustain demand, based largely on investment. Proposals of this kind have indeed been made. But they were not always put into effect. Soon, however, the completion of the large market will render coordination essential. It will also help achieve it, for the budget savings which will result from the opening up of public contracts will give the states more margin for manoeuvre. The European Left must be in the avant-garde of this strategy, without which we will have to pay too high a price economically, socially and politically for the Single Act.

We know that man today is capable both of mastering and of destroying nature. Given the risks threatening it, respect for the environment is the field *par excellence* of international action, for pollution pays no regard to customs officers or frontiers. The damage (to the air, the water, the landscape, etc.) is already considerable. We need harmonized rules so that environmental protection becomes a major objective everywhere, hand in hand with growth. This policy must become a major concern of the Left which, by definition, takes the long-term view and a wider view than the purely commercial one. The Europe we want to build – keeping a balance between tradition and modernity, technology and culture – must show the way to growth accompanied by respect for the environment.

B. FAIR COMPETITION

Macro-economic policies make it possible to accompany the opening up of Europe by other measures, and thus derive full benefit from it. Regulative policies, on the other hand, are designed to make it possible to correct the defects of the market. The definition of common juridical rules and the disappearance of the distortions resulting from public intervention should produce genuine competition.

First, the juridical rules. The completion of the internal market will be reflected by a speeding up in the number of mergers and take-overs, whether amicable or savage. These mergers are necessary to enable European undertakings to be competitive on the international market, vis à vis the Americans and the Japanese in particular. At the same time it must be ensured that the chances of growth through mergers are equal for all and that they do not fall to the cost of the consumer. The Community is already competent to control mergers, agreements and abuses of dominant position, but the instruments at its disposal are too rudimentary. It is time the Commission's endeavours to formulate a European competition law were successful.

Laying down rules in this area is indeed a delicate business. The ballast of sociology and the traditions of history weigh heavy in a Europe where we find every possible form, from undertakings whose capital is extremely tightly 'locked up' as in Germany, to those where it is very open as in Belgium. There are already national systems of rules, which are very heterogenous, and conflicts might well arise if they were maintained side by side with a European set of rules. The aim must be to determine the rules of the game clearly, rules governing all and which guarantee transparent transactions and equal status. Here too, precise and realistic objectives will have to be defined. Similarly, European company law must finally be defined, which will open the way to a European company statute.

51

Secondly, public intervention. The distortions of competition which result from systems of public aid to industry or company taxation must be wiped out. Public aid can, indeed, distort the play of market forces. So it is a good thing for the Community to try to limit it. However, this control must extend to all aid, national and local. Otherwise we would see even wider disparities between states, depending on how far they are decentralized. This control must also take account of national realities, that is to say it must not confuse public aid and the normal role of the state as shareholder in those states which have a nationalized sector. Aid can also have a positive influence on the play of the market, for the liberal mechanisms have proved ineffectual. It may in some cases be preferable to harmonize the various aid systems in view of a concerted industrial strategy rather than prohibit them: quite recently the Community was able to play a determinant part in the grant of aid for the restructuring of certain sectors. Can it want to mobilize resources for purposes of innovation while prohibiting aid for research and development? Collective consideration of the criteria of Commission control is required.

Taxation is an even more delicate matter. It needs a global, strategic and gradual approach. A global approach because the body of levies on undertakings affect the undertaking's cost and price formation and therefore determine the conditions of competition. Is it conceivable to harmonize VAT rates alone, without touching the tax on profits, investment taxation or social charges? The same applies to taxes on savings. If the movements of capital, which are taxed very differently in the various European countries, are liberalized, the free movement of savings will demand the harmonization of the levies on savings. Otherwise, the funds will be invested wherever the tax system is most favourable, which would create unacceptable imbalances.

It must be a strategic approach because a hesitant approach to harmonization would incur the risk of capital taxation adjusting downwards for the most 'liberal' systems and the taxation of labour adjusting upwards for the most 'socialized' systems: that would encourage financial speculation and discourage 'real' production. The European Left cannot want that kind of situation. So it must consider how to avoid this danger.

At the same time the approach has to be gradual: the disparities of situation and the diversity of tax and social systems are such that a step by step approach is the only possible one. VAT is an eloquent example. If the excessive disparities between countries remain, the disappearance of tax frontiers will be reflected by substantial differences in the price of one and the same product depending on the country of origin; inversely, immediate and total harmonization is difficult because of the wide spread of rates at present and because of the budgetary costs of any brusque adjustment.

So we must take the realistic road of a global and gradual rapprochement between the various tax systems, with the object of encouraging growth and on the basis of a definite and binding timetable, prior to the disappearance of the tax frontiers.

C. BALANCED INDUSTRIAL DEVELOPMENT

The implementation of the Single Act should avoid any risk of deindustrialization as a result of brutal and blind restructuring. The Left must promote the public authorities' activities in terms of encouraging a macro-economic approach and regulating the play of competition. It wants to see the public authorities alleviate any adverse effects and compensate for any weaknesses in the market. That is the role of a European industrial policy.

In that same spirit, we must seek first of all to eliminate certain adverse effects of the market, i.e. prevent Europe from developing in an unequal and imbalanced manner, which would strengthen the strong regions and further weaken the fragile zones. We must pursue special programmes for the regions whose development is lagging behind and programmes of conversion for declining regions. The decision to increase the resources allocated to the Community's structural funds was a necessary one. The sums involved are larger than those under the Marshall Plan! But we must also improve the conditions under which these resources are used, on the basis of a system of integrated projects to avoid any dispersion or duplication. Lastly, we must take account of the effects specifically attributable to the completion of the large market: for those areas or sectors affected by the restructuring that will result from the opening up of frontiers, it will be essential to formulate specific European follow-up and aid measures.

It is also up to the Left to promote a long-term systematic approach, something the market fails to do but which in fact determines the Community's future in economic competition. In the key sectors of the future, the combination of extremely concentrated investment, a continuous rise in productivity and soaring research and developing expenditure has given Japan considerable comparative advantages. They have enabled it to triple its manufacturing balance over a period of ten years, to the cost of the United States and Europe. The European countries did not stand by idly. They also embarked on a major endeavour, which led to the important ESPRIT and EUREKA programmes. The results are significant and are proof of a new way of thinking. From now on the technology battle will clearly require the participation of states, undertakings and research centres under flexible terms, and possibly even extending outside the confines of the Community.

This policy must be supplemented upstream by training, downstream by the spread of technology. For today everyone is aware how important training is for overall economic productivity: in Europe in the early 1980s only 28 per cent of a same class were likely to obtain a certificate giving them access to university, while the figure in the United States was 72 per cent and in Japan 87 per cent. In 1955, 20 per cent of Japanese students became workers, in 1965 the figure was 35 per cent and in 1983, 50 per cent. The European Left must endeavour to raise the general training level, improve technical training by forging closer links between the field of production and that of training,

54

and expand continuous training. This strategy calls for the harmonization of education systems. The mutual recognition of educational diplomas will help achieve this. It would also be useful to generalize the flexible European schemes of training loans and to expand the system of university exchanges based on the ERASMUS model. The European action programmes must also place emphasis on retraining for new occupations.

We must also endeavour to disseminate technological innovations, with the accompanying rises in productivity. The European countries' technology policy is suffering from a twofold handicap: it concentrates the financing on large undertakings and it gives precedence to 'high technology', which in France for instance picks up 90 per cent of state financing of industrial research and development. This kind of policy may well fail to see the role the less sophisticated industries can play in making the European economies more competitive. Obviously high technology is essential, but the other sectors account for some 90 per cent of industrial production, 80 per cent of exports, 95 per cent of employment. It may also underestimate the importance of disseminating information about innovations among the small traditional undertakings and the effectiveness of giving public aid to innovative SMEs.

There is, therefore, an urgent need to redirect the European countries' strategy of technological development towards the traditional sectors and the SMEs. The way has been pointed: wider access to public contracts, the formulation of specific programmes (why not consider an ESPRIT programme for the SMEs?), an increase in risk capital, making the public authorities responsible for the provision of organization and management advice.

D. A EUROPE OF SOCIAL DIALOGUE AND SOCIAL RIGHTS

When François Mitterand launched the idea of a social Europe in 1981, there were still some sceptical faces. Today everyone has realised that it is not just a market of 320 million consumers that is being built but a Europe of 320 million citizens and workers. The practical conclusions still need to be drawn, however: the need for a Europe of social rights and social dialogue.

A Europe of social rights: if national practices and legislations remain too disparate, Europe will not manage to superimpose any form of economic homogeneity on the excessive social disparities. If we genuinely want to build a Europe of competitive undertakings, we must build a Europe of human solidarity.

That presupposes the revival of one cornerstone of the employees' fundamental rights. The Commission has made progress in the harmonization of technical standards and in the field of health and safety. It must continue along that road and deal, for example, with employees' rights of expression and the terms of consultation with their employers. It is not a question of systematizing any one formula, but of establishing an area of convergence, a critical threshold below which it is not admissible to fall. The proposed European company statute, which offers various options and choices between different forms of employees' right of expression is an example of a pragmatic approach.

That also implies some degree of convergence between the systems of social redistribution. Once again it cannot be a question of brutally standardizing the levies and the benefits. But endeavours will have to be made to harmonize the different systems step by step. Otherwise undertakings would be established wherever the social levies are lowest and men would establish themselves where the benefits paid are highest. So we must start considering at this point how to set up a system of sluicegates between the various European approaches to allow the least advanced of them to develop. That is a major issue, and one which has not been fully perceived yet, of the completion of the internal market.

Lastly, it implies seeking to make the social policies more coherent. Now that most of the countries of Europe are facing similar situations – mass unemployment, especially among young people, social exclusion, immigration problems, etc. – it

56

would seem incomprehensible for them not to have any concerted policies. In a Europe which wants to be a single entity, surely we cannot accept too much inequality in terms of job precariousness? Is it conceivable for Europe to have as many immigration policies as it has countries? It would be desirable in the field of social action if comparisons between different experiences gave rise to collective projects and a common strategy.

Social dialogue is another item on the agenda. In their capacity of essential actors in the play of democracy and important factors of social cohesion, the unions have a role to play in the construction of Europe. But it is not an easy task to involve them. At a time when national dialogue, and even consultation at branch level, is tending to decline and give way to negotiations at enterprise level, it may seem unrealistic to try to create a forum that is even more remote from the real local situation. The diversity of European social history is reflected in the diversity of forms of workers' organization and of relations with employers. And, nearly everywhere, the trade union organizations are experiencing difficulties.

I would be tempted to say: all the more reason. The social dialogue can take on several forms: strengthening the Community consultation bodies, further efforts to establish what it has now been agreed to term the 'Val Duchesse dialogue', direct branch to branch relations within the Community. It is not possible to build a social Europe without the participation of the employees' organizations.

We must not miss the deadline on 31 December 1992 nor must we disappoint the hopes it is raising. The completion of the internal market will demand an immense effort, to transform structures and attitudes, to reorganize undertakings and retrain men. That prospect may look disturbing to those of our compatriots who are most exposed, those who have undergone the at times traumatic experience of modernization in recent years. If we are not careful, the original myth of Europe as a force for salvation could turn instead into a great fear.

So the Left must put forward a way of using the internal market that is based on the development of freedom and equality jointly: freedom of movement for men, goods and capital, equality between regions with regard to growth, between undertakings with regard to competition, between men with regard to training, employment and the redistribution of revenue.

That prospect presupposes a revival of state projects, which requires the modernization of the individual states and concerted efforts at European level on the basis of a common strategy. It also presupposes stronger democratic control by the European Parliament and the national parliaments and a more intensive social dialogue.

The initiatives of President François Mitterand, of Jacques Delors and many leading Socialists follow the same line. They show that the Left does not intend to stand idle before the risks, but above all before the opportunities for progress now facing the Europeans.

The social dimension: a political challenge

Felipe Gonzalez
Prime Minister (Spain)

INTRODUCTION

European integration is a challenge for all the citizens and institutions of the twelve Member States of the Community. It raises an essential question for politicians, namely how to combine the objectives of European construction with basic aims of another kind: a better distribution of income and of wealth, and a movement towards economic development characterized by greater equity and solidarity, whereby the rights of all citizens are protected.

In the process of European integration, the common industrial policy has for a long time been a matter of theoretical discussion: the need to establish Community legislation for industry, with wider implications concerning the appropriateness of State intervention in the economy. Where initiatives affecting the sector have been taken, they have in most cases been taken as a result of the development of other policies or in order to face up to specific problems. In the recent past, some of the efforts deployed have been devoted to satisfying the pressing needs for industrial readjustment in the sectors in which there is a crisis, in response to which all the Member States reacted by adopting different types of measures.

Today, we cannot escape the fact that national industrial restructuring policies have not yielded all the desired results. Despite the efforts of the various countries, Europe has still not reached appropriate levels of competitiveness in the traditional sectors on which that policy was focused, and the results of the action taken in the most advanced sectors, towards which we are being directed by the technical revolution, are as yet insufficient.

Our various countries should continue to make their own efforts, endeavouring to make them more effective day by day. We shall probably need to arm ourselves with a Community policy which, serving as a framework, will render national measures more productive and facilitate optimum utilization of the resources available.

All these problems are similar to those raised by the completion of the Internal Market in 1992, since in industrial policy there is a certain relationship of dependency. If the history of the Community is analysed, it will be seen that, although there was no specific policy for the industrial sector in the Treaty of Rome, the need for such a policy clearly emerged as soon as a degree of liberalization came about in trade between the six founding countries.

It is possible that the greatest efforts to accelerate the adoption of new Community industrial policy measures are now being made through decisions which will complete the Internal Market. These decisions are having clear repercussions upon employment.

The objective of achievement of the Internal Market presupposes a return to the original concept of the Common Market and it implies, according to the provisions of the Single Act, the creation of a single area without internal frontiers, in which there will be free and unhindered movement of persons, goods, services and capital.

However, considerable differences about the objective of the Internal Market exist between Member States, not unconnected from each state's position regarding the most beneficial type of European construction. Spain's Ministry of Industry and

Energy carried out a survey sampling 2,900 undertakings, which indicated a positive assessment of the Internal Market, regarded as beneficial both for undertakings and for the economy as a whole by the majority of those questioned.

As regards the obstacles which ought to be eliminated so that that objective can be attained, the most important areas mentioned were administrative customs procedures, rules governing transport, and the liberalization of capital and of public sector transactions. These are all specific areas, and in no case is there any doubt as to the need to achieve a more transparent and freer market as soon as possible.

As the first important amendment to the Treaties, the Single Act has created a new framework which has opened up new possibilities for European construction.

The enactment of the Single Act has brought important changes to Community order and is having clear repercussions on the institutional functioning and policies of the Community that have been applied since the birth of the Community. The area in which the Single Act makes the most profound change to the Treaties and establishes a new frontier is in its proposal for the simultaneous establishment of a series of new policies directed towards promoting the free movement of goods, services and capital, together with an outline of other policies designed to counter the negative effects upon the desired balance of economic development which might stem from the introduction of economic freedoms.

Any analysis of Community industrial policy must be seen in this context, in so far as that policy is designed to make the necessary changes to the machinery of production in order to improve the efficiency of industrial undertakings. This approach does not mean that industrial policy should be considered separately from general economic policy.

Industrial policy, as defined both in Community institutions and in each of the Member States, is very much affected by a particular set of circumstances from the 1970s. At that time, there was a need to react to the numerous changes brought about by the crisis, which, in addition to creating serious employment problems, resulted in a reduction of the role that each of the Member States plays on the international scene.

Also, the need to respond to the emerging situation brought about a substantial intervention in the economy by public administrations, which was closely related to industrial policy. This interventionism manifested itself in different ways from country to country, but was always combined with two types of action: measures of a national dimension designed to develop competitive capacity in sectors experiencing difficulty, and measures of regional policy intended to maintain activity in particular geographical areas. In addition, public deficits and the dubious effectiveness of public aid without specific aims must cause us to seek other channels through which to direct the implementation of an industrial policy.

The European Left must take on an active role in promoting a new industrial policy with advanced technological objectives, taking account of society's growing needs regarding the environment and quality of life.

There are clear signs that European industry has to some extent fallen behind its competitors, having been slow to adjust to the changes that have occurred at international level and to the patterns of trade in the last few years.

Among the reasons for this lack of progress are too few companies of sufficient size to face the increasing competition and the obstacles preventing the development of small and medium-sized undertakings, which, paradoxically, are adjusting readily to the introduction of high technology. Finally, there has been insufficient co-ordination, both in matters of research and in the incorporation of the results of research, in the new products put onto the market.

If the European industrial system is to be improved, there must be an improvement in the response to the problems mentioned above. For that purpose we should demonstrate the same capacity for co-ordination and planning as we showed in the periods of difficulty in order to ensure that the sectors in crisis regain a degree of viability.

It is also action of this type that constitutes the embryo of a common positive industrial policy, which is so necessary from the social point of view in order to eliminate the negative connotations associated with the restructuring measures. An example of the paths we must follow in order to achieve development can be found in the common scientific and technological development programmes, where there already exists a degree of co-ordination of national programmes and policies. It is thus necessary to operate on a European scale for the purpose of certain industrial measures which, by promoting greater co-operation and co-ordination between the Member States, will increase our competitiveness internationally.

Nevertheless, promotion of the Community industrial policy must be undertaken with caution, since the individual industrial structures of the Member States differ considerably and there are substantial differences between the infrastructures available to companies, depending upon the areas in which they are located. This does not require us to maintain protective measures between the Member States, to be used whenever difficulties appear in a particular sector or geographical area. On the contrary, the solution to problems must be found immediately, not for the short term but rather to find stable and enduring solutions, by according to social problems and to regional balance the same status we accord to the initiatives designed to achieve the Internal Market.

Against that background, the Internal Market for 1992 is an opportunity to create a true Community social and economic area, with freedom of trade, improved living and working conditions and the highest possible level of employment.

For a more balanced Europe, the Single Act aims for economic and social cohesion, which must not be based solely on special financial effort or upon temporary measures that relate above all to new member countries. The cohesion must extend to all Community policies and incorporate in them the requisite consistency and equilibrium.

A central objective for the European Left, and indeed for every European of conviction, is that the result of the Single Act should be the creation of an internal economic area without frontiers and a social fabric that will enable European integration to make genuine advances.

The Single Act, whose innovations render this new approach possible, highlights the need for extending the social dimension of Europe, which was already referred to in the founding Treaties. The need to progress in social matters has prompted the European Commission to adopt a series of initiatives, setting out specific objectives designed to give social content to the Internal Market.

The harmonization of national legislation on social matters, should lead to the drafting of Community rules governing the fundamental areas of labour relations and the employment market, and ensuring recognition of basic rights, both individual and collective. Thus, within this logical framework of political compromise intended to ensure advancement in the process of European integration, our position is one of total support for the objective of the Internal Market by 1992.

The Spanish position has always been favourable to substantial progress with reforms, tempered by full awareness that the scope of reforms cannot be limited to an increase in freedom of competition, but must be more ambitious in extending the frontiers of European integration, having regard to each and every one of the factors incorporated in the Single Act. I feel that it is essential for European construction to refer to the political importance of the Single Act and all its implications. It must be remembered that the European Council at its Milan meeting in June 1985 rejected the aim desired by many, namely that of laying the constitutional foundation for European union. The Single Act, that is to say the institutional reforms, the Internal Market, the social area, cohesion and the other new policies, constitutes one step further along the road towards that objective, but in no case must it be confused with the objective itself. By reason of the very fact that it is incomplete, the Single Act should be seen as a measure that will be overtaken by other new initiatives in the process of integration.

As far as the reform of institutional machinery is concerned, the balance sheet is encouraging, by reason of changes introduced by the Single Act and of developments in the decision-making process of the Community. But the scope of the Internal Market is not so great as originally proposed by the Commission. Important matters have been exempted from voting by a qualified majority and there are restrictions of indubitable importance, such as the possibility of recourse to Article 36. However, the adoption of 1992 as the target date will provide a great stimulus for the adoption of the nearly three hundred proposals for regulations and directives contained in the Commission's White Paper and will inevitably render certain progress essential in all the policies that make up the Community patrimony.

The idea of economic and social cohesion in the Community, which we must define together in accordance with the needs and stages of implementation of various policies, is in itself an undoubted success. But at the same time it is true that the manner in which cohesion has been formulated, without defined financial resources appropriated to it, falls far short of the ideal solution that we would have liked to see. There are now grounds for hope that the creation of a European social area will bring substantial improvements in working conditions. To that end, a degree of harmonization in working conditions must be introduced in the twelve Member States as a first step forward.

The basic question inherent in the implementation of the Single Act is the relationship between the opening up of the market, accompanying social measures and economic and social cohesion. As the experience of the Community itself has shown, the process of liberalizing trade may carry with it both positive effects, such as increases in productivity, and adverse effects which frustrate attainment of the desired national or regional balances or hinder the advancement of particular social issues.

We are moving towards a new industrial society, motivated both by the dynamism generated by our relations within the Community itself, and by international events, in which we simultaneously play both an active and a passive role. Liberalization of our market is a precondition for enhanced freedom of competition and, in consequence, greater productivity on the part of our companies. If we are to control the adverse effects stemming from this process, we must for the time being adopt a cautious approach in applying the rules of free competition, having regard to the differing levels from which progress must start in each geographical area. There must indeed be temporary exemptions, to be superseded in the medium term in step with the results gradually obtained from the follow-up policies incidental to the Internal Market.

The Single Act, a legislative instrument of the same rank as the Treaty of Rome, lays down the objectives of cohesion and creation of a social area, putting them on exactly the same level as the remainder of the Community objectives. It is, therefore, the best guarantee that the process of European integration will continue, that we shall take account of all matters upon which the balance and well-being of society are based.

Towards social and economic renewal in Europe

Wim Kok
Labour Party Leader (The Netherlands)

THE CHALLENGE

Western Europe and European policy face challenges. How will they respond to mass unemployment? Will Europe be able to hold its own in competition with the United States, Japan and the newly industrialising countries? How will new technology influence our future? What does the future hold for the natural environment in which we live? These are four separate questions, but they cannot be asked separately from each other, and answers to them are needed. This paper takes the broad challenge of the 1990s as its starting-point and looks at the social, economic and technological modernization of Europe. On the economic and technological fronts competition from the US and Japan is readily apparent. There is more talk than ever before of a single world market. Today's big companies might have their headquarters in particular countries, but they are in essence transnationals with branches and subsidiaries on various continents, as modern transport and communications technologies make distances and times shorter.

This increase in the scale of production and finance poses a challenge to both national and European policy. International competition means that progress with economic integration within the Community is of great importance. This process

67

places new responsibilities upon social democrats. The first is to ensure that the modernization of the European economy also comprises the necessary social progress. The second is to build a genuinely European outlook in the social-democratic parties of western Europe. If this does not happen, the ability to direct and coordinate in the economy, technology and the environment will to a large extent will be lost.

In 1986 the Community countries decided that the internal market would be completed in 1992. This new spur towards economic integration in the Community initially turned out to be less powerful than had been hoped. But in 1988 '1992 fever' struck, and major steps have now been taken towards the free movement of people, money and goods.

Europe's social democrats have played an active part in bringing about this much-needed acceleration in economic integration. They have also played a major part in devising programmes to encourage the development and use of new technology. It is now high time for us to give a powerful and well-planned boost to *social* modernization in Europe.

I do not intend to discuss social modernization as though it *contrasted* with economic and technological modernization. I wish to make it clear that social modernization is a vital component of successful modernization of the European economy. Europe's social democrats must as a matter of urgency launch new initiatives to bring about a sounder form of social and economic modernization in the Community. We must develop a joint policy that will both strengthen the economic and technological base of industry in the Member States and solve a number of pressing social problems. Social democrats in all the Member States have taken a number of steps to bring about this kind of balanced economic modernization. Now we must channel our energies into bringing together and combining national plans.

Wim Kok

From time to time slightly panic-stricken stories appear in the European media suggesting that Europe is losing the battle of economic and technological competition with Japan and the US. The interesting thing is that precisely the same prophecies of doom about 'our competitive position' are being made by the media in the United States and Japan. So Europeans are not alone in worrying about their economic future. And this is understandable: at a time of rapid technological development the competitive position of companies and industries is constantly at risk, both in Europe and elsewhere.

Every company in every country in the world now faces far more and far greater uncertainties than it did some twenty years ago. Production methods and markets are changing rapidly. Advances in process automation and control are likely to make possible fundamental changes in business strategy, away from economies of scale towards specialization and economies of scope. Various new technologies (such as microelectronics and biotechnology) are increasingly blurring the destinctions between different products and industries, and this is sharpening competition. On top of this, advances in transport and telecommunications are accelerating the movement of goods and information, forcing management to respond faster to market changes. The instability brought by these technological trends is enhanced by the failure of western governments satisfactorily to coordinate economic and financial policy, and this has led to wild fluctuations in interest and exchange rates.

For individual firms this can bring both major threats and huge opportunities. The prevailing feeling in Europe is an exaggerated fear that we will be the victims of accelerated technological change. I would not claim the Community economy does not have its weak points, or that there are no direct threats to the competitiveness of particular industries in the Member States. The problems are there, and they must be tackled energetically by governments and the two sides of industry. But we must not sink into pessimism about the resilience of the European economy and its potential for growth.

The Community is a group of countries with relatively high per capita income, a well educated labour force and highly developed physical, social and scientific infrastructure. If despite this strong starting position we do not manage to continue to play a leading role in the world economy, it will not be because there is something fundamentally wrong with the structure of out economy and our society, but because we are unable to exploit to the full the major opportunities they offer.

MORE THAN JUST HI-TECH

In all the Community countries efforts to modernize have hitherto been focussed on a limited number of technologies that are seen as the most advanced and the most promising: microelectronics, telecommunications, biotechnology and new materials. All the European countries have chosen virtually the same list of priorities, even those whose economic strength is based mainly on other industries. In The Netherlands, for example, whose agricultural sector has deceloped into one of the most productive and highest-exporting in the world, farming is still not seen as a hi-tech industry.

This fixation – for such it is – on the same old advanced industrial technologies has produced an industrial policy that seeks primarily to encourage leading-edge research by the largest European companies in those industries. In itself this is not necessarily unproductive, provided that adequate conditions are attached to this support.

But the policy must not be restricted to support for research by these large companies. One of the important features of the new technologies is that they can be used in a wide range of applications in virtually every sector of the economy. The speed and success of their spread is ultimately as important to the economic health of a country or a continent as remaining at the frontiers of technology.

In France, to take an example, there has been a traditional emphasis in socialist thinking about the structure of industry on the way individual companies and industries link to form clusters of economic activity. This approach leads to the conclusion that one-sided concentration on the biggest companies and the most advanced 'sunrise' industries must be avoided, because it can mean that small and medium-sized firms are neglected or important opportunities to regenerate the 'sunset' industries are missed. And above all that the huge strength and potential of industries that are flourishing – the 'sunshine industries' – are ignored. Support for the front-runners in the most advanced European industries – however justified in itself – must not be accompanied by neglect of the rest of the economy. Member State and Community economic policy at present concentrates too much on the development of new technology and too little on its application. Generally speaking far too little attention is given to finding the best social environment in which to apply new technologies, even though this plays a large part in determining whether innovations will succeed or fail.

THE SOCIAL DIMENSION OF MODERNIZATION

An IBM Netherlands manager said recently that the automation of companies and institutions was 10% computer hardware, 20% software and 70% organizational change. The development and application of new technology in companies and institutions is still seen predominantly as a *technical* process, whereas in fact it is much more a *social* process. This is borne out every day in the many companies and institutions that go through the trauma of computerization. Many of these failures are the direct result of an approach to computerization in which social and organizational factors are seen as peripheral and considered only after the technical specifications for the project have been finalized.

A similar, observation can be made about the broader social 'infrastructure' within which a company operates. Comparisons of companies in different countries working with the same technology and the same machines show that there can be differences in productivity of up to 60%. These are brought about to a large extent by worker-management relations within companies and the strength of the industrial base. Contrary to popular belief, the productivity of a firm or industry depends primarily not on the quality of its machinery, but on how the hardware is used. A whole range of social and institutional changes are needed if society is to be able to work with the new technology productively and in a socially acceptable way.

European companies are not in themselves any less well equipped than their competitors, and the vast majority of European companies are not lagging behind in skills or research – in many cases they are ahead. The obvious conclusion is that we must work towards a technology policy that takes seriously the social and institutional environment in which technology is introduced and used.

A considerable amount of research is still needed in this area. At present enormous sums are spent on the (technical) development of new technologies, while the social and political circumstances in which a given technology can be used the most productively receive only minimal attention. We must end this absurd imbalance.

A modernization strategy must involve investing not only in technology but also in developing automation-related skills. More effective cooperation must be developed between technical universities and researchers in the human and social sciences. This will allow issues concerning the implications of automation for the distribution and organization of work, the type of management that is needed and the most appropriate scale of automation to be addressed.

CHARACTERISTICS OF EUROPE

Inasmuch as the social implications of modernization are taken seriously at all in the European countries, in conservative quar-

72

ters they are usually viewed in an extremely one-sided way. The social structure of the European countries and the network of relations within their populations are presented as barriers to further economic and technological progress. The second obstacle that is still emphasised in some quarters is the 'fragmentation' of the European market. There are indeed substantial economic and social differences between countries and regions within western Europe. Our entire culture is permeated by them. But do they constitute barriers to our economic and technological development? Less and less. The more the old economies of scale are replaced by economies of scope as a result of technological development, the more easily manufacturers are able to serve large numbers of different markets.

Industries that have already invested on a large scale in flexible automation of production are more readily able to tailor mass production to individual customer requirements. However, the existence of a large, undivided and homogeneous market remains important for the economical manufacture of mass-produced goods and for small and medium-sized firms.

The path being taken by technological development must be combined with the completion of the internal market. Europe's diversity of cultures, lifestyles and products can make it economically stronger and more attractive, particularly if we make the effort to increase contact and communication between the societies of the individual Member States. The Erasmus project is a good example of a European programme that could boost contact between the different societies.

The fact that European governments intervene fairly substantially in their economies and in the distribution of income offers all kinds of opportunities for boosting social innovation. There are large and relatively easily identifiable government markets in many sectors of the European economy. This situation must not be changed. On the contrary – it must be exploited, in the same way as the United States – in what is perhaps a slightly odd analogy – consciously uses the defence budget to stimulate certain sectors of the economy. This kind of action will do much more to induce European industry to use its creativity to move towards social innovation. One outstanding example is the mushrooming of R&D in ergonomics and workplace safety in the Scandinavian countries in response to tough legislation that has constantly been tightened up. Virtually all the western European countries have now (very belatedly) adopted the standards developed in Scandinavia. A number of Scandinavian companies have been able to translate the skills in ergonomics and safety learned as a result of government policy into high-quality, internationally recognized products.

TOWARDS A NEW BLUEPRINT FOR SOCIETY IN EUROPE

The consensus between employers, employees and government that fostered economic growth and brought fair distribution of its benefits is now disintegrating, at least in the form it took in the fifties and sixties (and which was known as Fordism), as a result of social and technological change.

It is beyond dispute that trends can now be seen in society and the economy that are having a detrimental effect on industrial relations in Europe. The most obvious example is the continuing high unemployment in the Community countries, which affects different groups within the working population to sharply differing extents. Another is the threat that workforces will be fragmented as a result of the flexible automation discussed above. This fragmentation could lead to the collapse of collective employment agreements into collections of individual contracts. These two trends could undermine the position of unions and bodies within companies that involve workers in decisionmaking and make it easier for employers to introduce more authoritarian management methods.

Calls are currently being heard on the right for fundamental reforms in industrial relations. It is claimed that in the long term the Community countries can only hold their own against international competition if they decide now to mimic every feature of Japanese and American industrial relations. This would amount to a move towards authoritarian corporatism *à la japonaise*, or towards a much tougher and more divided society *à la* United States. A hardening of the climate in society of this kind is not only undesirable from the social point of view, but would also adversely affect the competitive position of Community industry. There are major differences between the Community countries where industrial relations – the relations between employers, employees, unions and government – are concerned. But compared with the United States and Japan there are more similarities than differences. Efforts have been made over the last few decades in all the European countries to build up a social security and welfare system in which government plays an important regulatory and supportive role. In addition, there is far greater emphasis in industrial relations throughout Europe on consultation between the two sides of industry, worker consultation and worker involvement in decision-making than is found in Japan or the United States. The main reason why we as social democrats have no sympathy for the adoption of even parts of the American or Japanese system is of course that for many people this would adversely affect incomes, job security and involvement in their company's management. Not only would it be extremely difficult to shift industrial relations in one of these two directions, but such a shift would be accompanied by a serious weakening of the social fabric of our countries. To copy these models would be to surrender the unique features of our own model, from which more than ever before we must draw our strength.

Attempts to make fundamental changes in the present system of industrial relations in the European countries and to push them in the direction of a 'confrontational' American or Japanese system will come to nothing. But we are already seeing that they are considerably undermining the willingness to tackle our economic and social problems in a concerted way.

Social democrats now face the challenge of giving substance to a new system of industrial relations that takes Europe further down the road towards the type of society that is right for it.

The fact that in many European companies the introduction of new technology is not going very smoothly, or that too little innovation is taking place, is often blamed on the workforce or the bodies that represent it, as though technological advance in Europe were stagnating because there is too much worker involvement in decision-making.

In most cases the cause of this stagnation is in fact to be found less in resistance from below than in a lack of cooperation from above – namely when management gives far too little attention during the process of modernization to informing and consulting its workforce, gradual changes in the skills required of them, in-house training and organizational changes. These changes take longer than installing an advanced machine, but the machine will not work efficiently until there has been a measure of organizational change and the workers affected genuinely accept the new equipment. Many obstacles to modernization in companies and institutions, and many traumatic experiences, could be avoided by greater worker involvement. I believe large numbers of employers would be prepared to give their complete agreement to broad involvement by staff and their organizations in the process of modernization. Our efforts must be directed towards ensuring that this involvement is not restricted to the workers whom management considers to be essential for the smooth operation of the company.

The second vital area where broad agreement must be reached between workers, employers and government is training. At present there is an enormous need for appropriate training, both for people whose skills are outdated and for groups whose present skills mean that they have few job prospects. With the advent of advanced production systems, companies are attaching more and more importance to workers' skills, flexibility and ability to work independently. The quality of work is going to be an increasingly topical issue in this context. Companies increasingly feel obliged to keep their remaining staff, who often have highly responsible jobs and operate sensitive, expensive equipment, with the company by making working conditions as pleasant as possible.

But training and job enrichment must not be available only to people who already occupy relatively strong positions within their companies. Other groups of people both in and out of work have at least as much right to such opportunities. In fact training schemes should improve the job prospects of women, members of minority groups, the long-term unemployed and other groups of people who are 'less attractive' to employers. We must find ways of making sure that the increased effort being put into training does not simply strengthen the trend towards segmentation of the labour market and ultimately the much-feared divided society. This requires active government mediation and intervention.

REDISTRIBUTION OF WORK

If we are to find answers to the major social problems facing the Community today, we must bring together three areas of policy.

Firstly, we must find ways of giving the technological modernization that is necessary a positive and progressive direction. Secondly, we must try to satisfy the enormous training needs of both the employed and the unemployed. Thirdly, we must at all costs prevent the current trend towards labour market segmentation leading to there being one group in the population with prospects and another with none. Redistribution of work will be essential in this task: the shortage of jobs for the Community's (still growing) workforce is just too big. In addition to this, paid and unpaid work must also be redistributed.

There are ways of killing all three birds with one stone, for example introducing different kinds of training leave. After a certain number of years in a job, people could have the opportunity to take training leave, possibly with an obligation to concentrate on new technological developments in their specialist area. The job made available could be temporarily filled by a (long-term) unemployed person, who could be given the necessary training. Such a scheme would increase skill levels and promote redistribution of work. This example shows that it is possible to devise measures that would make a positive contribution to solving social problems while at the same time strengthening the economy.

THE QUALITY OF LIFE

All the major electronics companies in Europe, the US and Japan are currently engaged in the race to produce the first high-definition television. These large, pin-sharp screens are due to come on to the market at the beginning of the 1990s, and once they are available many people will undoubtedly want to have one. But is it right that so much research capacity should be used just for a product like this, when so many basic human needs remain unmet, both in Europe and in the rest of the world?

Too often social progress is still seen as a chance by-product of technical and economic progress. European industry is still fixated on a group of well-off consumers, even though other large markets could be tapped. Research in The Netherlands shows that there is considerable demand for specially designed domestic appliances for the elderly. Industry is still not interested in this group, even though society is ageing and an increasing proportion of the national income is being spent on them.

The same applies to new pollution control technology and the development of appropriate technology for the Third World. Our basic principle must be that the benefits of technological development must not be enjoyed only by the rich and the powerful. And this means we must devise strategies for making the quality of life for the bulk of the population the main focus of technological development.

Making the quality of life our central concern means introducing social and environmental criteria into a process of evaluation that all too often at present short-sightedly takes notice only of strictly economic factors. This is no simple matter.

It is not enough simply to lay down basic groundrules for economic and technological modernization. We must try to change the underlying direction of research and product development, and this will require considerable effort.

If social and environmental criteria are to be given greater weight in the modernization process, we must copy Europe's successful space programme and launch a 'space programme for society'. This must identify the social, political and environmental problems that we believe can and must be solved by technological advances. Such a European programme would be an excellent framework for R&D by companies and institutions, and it could set in motion a wave of new economic activity.

I have written to the President of the Commission, Jacques Delors, calling for a European Technology and Employment Agency to be set up. The remit of this body could include collecting and pooling information on research and practical experience.

Making the quality of life our central concern also means finding ways of dealing with the dangers threatening all life: weapons and environmental problems. It is becoming increasingly clear that economic development is underpinned by ecological balance, and this involves not just pollution in a narrow sense – e.g. illegal dumping of toxic waste – but equally broader links between the environment, the economy and technology.

Economic growth is placing increasing strain on resources, energy and land. A commission headed by the Norwegian premier Gro Harlem Brundtland recently produced a report on this subject called 'Our Common Future'. The report's main theme is sustainable development, and this will call for changes in production and production processes. New technologies can help: products can be manufactured using less energy and fewer resources. New investment should be channelled specifically into environmental improvement technology. This means that the right choices must be made – the right technology and the right investment. Obviously government must play a part by providing the right framework and offering investment incentives, and by investing itself, for example in energy conservation.

THE EUROPEAN COMMUNITY

The Community is not seen in either The Netherlands or the other Member States as a necessary and useful engine of the social and economic changes we seek. This lack of enthusiasm is to a large extent the result of the unsatisfactory nature of the Community's institutional structure. The European Parliament can monitor and influence the Commission but not the Council, which is alongside and above the Commission. The Council, the ultimate decision-making body, in which the thorniest problems have to be resolved, can only be attacked at the national level, within the individual Member States. It is virtually impossible from within the Member States to force it to take new initiatives and to develop exciting policies.

This history of the economic cooperation strategy for the Member States proposed by the Commission in 1986 illustrates this point. The strategy comprises three complementary components:

- national governments are to ensure that demand is sufficient to make possible faster growth in the economy and in employment;
- employers are to invest more;
- the unions are to help to keep pay increases under control, leading to moderate increases in real terms.

All the governments agreed on these basic principles, and in November 1986 they were endorsed by the European umbrella organizations representing employers and workers. But there is minimal commitment in the Member States to implementing this common strategy. There is a clear lack of political willingness to make any changes to national policy as a result of European-level agreements, and conversely steps taken in the individual Member States do not give rise to a common approach.

In 1988 this stagnation in cooperation within the Community was to some extent overcome. After lengthy negotiations an agreement was reached in the Council in February 1988 that will control agricultural spending and combat overproduction in the sector. At the same time it was decided in due course (in 1993) to double social and regional structural policy funding. This is particularly important for the countries with weaker economies, such as the southern European countries and Ireland. The Commission rightly established linkage between sorting out the Community's finances, increasing the structural funds and the completion of the internal market. The economic disparities in the Community mean that the liberalization of the movement of goods, money, services and people must be accompanied by a structural policy to strengthen the weaker regions.

Interest in 1992 is mounting significantly in the Community countries. Rosy visions and gloom-laden predictions abound: rosy visions of production and sales in the biggest consumer market in the world, with 320 million people, and gloom-laden predictions about the consequences of tougher international competition and the less of national sovereignty. Now that the initial dust has settled, we should look more soberly at the opportunities offered by 1992 and the conditions that should be attached to it. The relationship between national and European policy must be examined. Three main points emerge from this examination.

The first concerns the internal market in the narrow sense. The Commission's White Paper is based on the Single Act and identifies the physical, technical and fiscal barriers that will have to be removed to achieve freedom of movement. This is an important process that will open up opportunities, but it has its pitfalls – such as the harmonization of excise duties and indirect taxation.

Secondly, the process of building the internal market, which offers so much, is clearly not enough in itself. It will create opportunities and potential for economic progress. These must be exploited and used if the goals of welfare improvements and reductions in unemployment are to be achieved. This is emphasised by the report of the Cecchini commission on the economic implications of the internal market. At its congress in Lisbon in May 1987 the Federation of Socialist Parties in the Community also set out a policy in which targetted stimulation of the economy by (government) investment in physical and social infrastructure occupies an important place.

But economic cooperation between the Member States should not cause them to turn their backs on the rest of the world. On the contrary, Europe has an important part to play in tackling the imbalances in the world economy and the North-South divide. The Community countries must work energetically both individually and collectively to solve the problem of the debt that is imposing such a burden on a large group of developing countries. We must guard against the creation of an internal market that has high(er) barriers around its perimeter, as this would seriously restrict the Third World's trade opportunities.

Thirdly, European cooperation in the 1990s must not be confined to 'negative' integration (removing barriers) and economic issues. More positive, specific forms of integration are necessary if the Europe of 1992 is genuinely to be a Europe of qualitative progress – namely European technology, environmental and social policy. The Single Act expands the Community's brief some way along this path, but more radical initiatives are needed.

The social blueprint for Europe outlined above calls for a European social policy. Social innovation and progress mean that where social security is concerned, the systems developed in the northern European countries should set the standard. We must work to see that the other countries grow towards this, for example by means of regularly reassessed minimum standards. The only possible harmonization is harmonization upwards. We need a directive, based on the Single Act, laying down requirements for health and safety in the workplace. The internationalization of business must be paralleled by substantive action on the rights of workers and their representatives to information and involvement in decision-making across national borders.

European-level consultation between employers and workers must be energetically promoted.

The importance of the social dimension of European cooperation was highlighted in the summer of 1988, partly thanks to the European Trade Union Confederation, and partly thanks to the Commission under the leadership of Jacques Delors. In September 1988 the Commission published an important document entitled 'The Social Dimension of the Internal Market'. Active input by social democrats in this area is one of our main tasks in the coming months.

The question is how this process of integration can be carried out in such a way that grassroots enthusiasm is not stifled at birth. The idea that European integration will amount to no more than further centralization of decision-making is frequently heard. This is a dangerous misconception. Of course it is true that further political integration of the Community will mean a major shift of powers from individual countries to Europe. But this certainly does not have to mean that there will be a new tier of government that is completely inaccessible to the individual citizen, at least if greater efforts are made to decentralize and differentiate policy, and particularly its implementation.

The social-democratic parties in Europe have always pressed for 'functional decentralization' of decision-making: where possible, decision-making power must be transferred from central institutions to lower levels in the system. New technologies offer the potential for further improvements in the quality of decentralized, autonomous decision-making in the regions, for example by giving those involved access to more and better information.

As political integration moves ahead, we must seek to ensure that more direct links are established between local and regional institutions and the Community. Here and there moves in this direction can already be seen. The integrated programmes for the Mediterranean countries already include direct contact between the regions concerned and the Commission. This trend could mean that powers are transferred from national governments either to Europe or to the regions. We should use these opportunities to make the structure of government in our countries simpler and more straightforward.

CONCLUSION

In all the Community countries governments and the two sides of industry are wrestling with the same problems: disappointing economic growth, mass unemployment, government budget deficits, stagnant investment by industry, the threat of a new wave of poverty, widening regional disparities and attacks on the environment. But the seriousness of these problems, and the fact that they are affecting all the Member States equally, are still generating far too few exciting initiatives in European policy. Social-democrats are the political force to breathe new life into the dormant process of European unification and to give it a progressive direction.

But even the social-democratic parties in Europe do not yet grasp sufficiently clearly the potential for new political initiatives in Europe. They focus their attention exclusively on national politics and relegate Europe to the bottom of their agenda. This must change. The increase in the scale of social and economic development means that political activity must be conducted on a European scale. If it is not, considerable scope for influencing, directing and coordinating will be lost. Concrete cooperation between the social-democratic parties in the Community must be tackled more energetically. The question of whether moves should be made towards the formation of a European party should be addressed.

We stand before the challenge of formulating a joint blueprint for the responsible modernization of Europe. The tasks before us are clear and urgent: economic growth, job creation and finding an ecological balance. The building blocks for the blueprint already exist. For the sake of the future of Europe we must work for practical reform and keep our sights set clearly on the 1990s.

The challenge of 1992

Hans-Jochen Vogel
President of the SPD (West Germany)

I CREATING A EUROPEAN SOCIAL AREA

THE SENSE OF NEW DEPARTURE IN EUROPE AND SCEPTICISM

The feeling of weariness with Europe that characterized the 1970s and was widespread until recent times has given way to a sense of a new departure in Europe. The aim of creating a 'Europe without internal frontiers' by 31 December 1992, agreed by the twelve Member States of the Community and set out in the Single European Act which came into force on 1 July 1987, is increasingly dominating the thinking, planning and behaviour of undertakings. The growing number of mergers between undertakings and co-operation agreements is a clear sign that the economy is adjusting to the internal market, to 'Europe 1992'.

The trade unions are also in favour of the completion of the internal market and are preparing for it. Like the Social Democratic Party of Germany, however, they have always linked their assent to the demand that the social effects of the internal market must also be taken into consideration and the market must develop into a European social area.

There are reasons for this. The economically weaker Community countries fear that the opening up of the markets will mainly benefit the more industrialized states and only exacerbate their own labour market problems. But a similar concern can also be found in the more industrialized states, especially among employees working in economic sectors which were specially protected in the past. They too fear that sharper competition following the opening up of the borders will put their jobs at risk without creating any prospect of new ones. It is not possible to forecast which states and regions will emerge from 'Europe 1992' as winners and which as losers. In the Commission's view, which can be accepted, Europe as a whole will gain new jobs as a result of the completion of the internal market. But obviously that is no consolation to those who will become the victims of sharper competition and rationalization.

These anxieties could be allayed if only Europe could resolve itself to make a common European effort to promote employment, as the Commission has been proposing since 1985 in its 'Co-operative Strategy for Growth and Employment'. So far the forces of conservatism in Europe have refused to endorse the kind of co-operative strategy, but we European Social Democrats and Socialists must continue to press for it.

There is also a certain scepticism about 'Europe 1992' because there is no indication to date that it will be a Europe of social progress. Quite the contrary. There is a risk that we will see a Europe of capital based on the lowest common denominator. Representatives of industry, and conservative politicians, too, see 'Europe 1992' as the greatest deregulation measure in economic history. That description should not frighten us, for an internal market without frontiers quite simply means 'deregulation' in the sense of removing the barriers to the free movement of goods, people, services and capital.

What is frightening for us, however, is that capitalist circles quite evidently regard 'Europe 1992' as a chance to undermine or 'deregulate' social achievements.

In order to remove alleged disadvantages in competition they want to reduce the taxes on business earnings, disregard environmental demands, develop supposedly cheap nuclear energy, lengthen working hours, weaken social security systems and hold back wages even more. They also hope to ease 'excessive' safety and health rules, to delete some workers' protection rights and undermine the co-determination and co-decision-making rights of workers and their union representatives.

These demands are based on an approach which relegates high standards of protection, safety rules and the social rights of workers to mere cost factors and parameters which can be reduced at any time for economic reasons. It forgets that workers' health protection, a good level of training and a high level of social stability, based mainly on the social protection and rights that workers have struggled for over a period of decades, are not disadvantages but on the contrary very definite advantages, which contribute to the success of a country's economy. The Federal Republic of Germany and the Netherlands with their comparatively high social welfare standards are impressive evidence of this.

GATHERING STRENGTH

Ernst Breit, President of the European Trade Union Confederation and Chairman of the German Trade Union Federation, was therefore right to warn against 'introducing a deregulation campaign against social rights under the pretext of completing the European internal market'. He pointed out that 'the completion of the European internal market must not become the Trojan Horse used by conservatives who want to change the system and turn back the wheel of history'.

So the question of how to prevent the erosion of hard-won social rights concerns us all. It calls for a clear and common response on the part of all the Social Democratic parties of Europe. That clear answer has not been given yet. But it is high time we found it and used all our combined strength to create a

European social area together with the European internal market, in which technical and economic progress goes hand in hand with social progress.

In its European social programme entitled 'Creating the European social area in the internal market' of February 1988, the European Trade Union Confederation points the way we European Social Democrats and Socialists must follow in company with the trade unions. Our aim cannot be to standardize all the social provisions in Europe. The traditional historical differences between specific requirements and options are too great for that. The economically weaker regions of the Community could not cope with the harmonization of social provisions at the highest level, and that would immediately destroy the impetus to growth created by the completion of the internal market. Any harmonization at middle level would also face the weaker regions with economic difficulties, while signifying an unjustifiable reduction in social rights for the socially advanced regions. The road to a European social area can, therefore, only mean convergence on a basis of progress, gradually reducing differences and improving social welfare overall.

It is up to the Social Democratic parties and the unions jointly to bring about step-by-step improvements in the European social system, which is only sketched out in the present EEC Treaty and the Single European Act. Europe must not be a Europe of businessmen – it must become a Europe of social progress!

We must also remember that the social structures of Europe are changing rapidly. While the services sector is growing at the cost of the production sector, the ratio of employees is also growing while the ratio of the workers is falling. Part-time work is also on the increase. At the same time we are witnessing a trend towards individualization. Partly as a result of better training, an increasing number of people are freeing themselves from their traditional ties and backgrounds and making their own decisions about the way to lead and plan their lives. This applies in particular to women, who are calling for an end to dated role concepts and full equal status and rights – and not just in working life. Increasingly short working hours also promote individualization.

This trend involves risks and opportunities. It can lead to the dissolution of solidary communities and thereby further increase the power of the owners of capital. It can split society into a majority whose well-being continues to increase and a minority which lags behind and is gradually marginalized, especially at times when economic growth as a whole is weak and unemployment is correspondingly high.

But that same trend can improve the quality of life of all concerned and increase the sense of responsibility of the individual, without destroying the bonds of solidarity which create more humane working processes and bring us closer to the kind of society in which the principles of democracy also apply to the economy, and in which labour is no longer in the service of capital, but capital is at last in the service of labour.

Which of these two variants becomes reality largely depends on whether we leave things to develop by themselves or whether we can influence the direction and impose social and ecological criteria – i.e. whether the forces which want to and can influence this development are strong enough. That means strengthening the European Confederation of Trade Unions, which must in future secure itself far more respect at European level as a factor of power. The same applies to the Social Democratic and Socialist parties in the Community, whose hitherto rather loose association must be built up into a political decision-making centre. That implies an increase in the Confederation's staffing and the transition to majority decisions.

II MAKING EUROPE MORE EFFICIENT

DEFINING THE AIMS

We must also apply all our creative force in an attempt to evolve a European industrial policy that represents more than a mere abstract increase in the efficiency of industry and the economy – i.e. a policy which also looks to the aims of technical and economic developments and tries to influence the directions of development. In our view there is no question that we need this kind of industrial policy at European level, a policy in fact that is geared to humane and ecological criteria. It is equally obvious to us that industrial policy must be embedded in the European social area that we are going to develop step-by-step, so as to ensure that every section of the population can enjoy the fruits of technical and economic progress.

The supporters of economic 'laisser-faire' regard any attempt by the state to influence technical and economic trends as 'a sin against the spirit of the market economy'. We are not afraid of such reproaches, remote as they are from reality. For the state always has and still does influence technical trends – by its infrastructure policy, its procurements, by its lax or strict environmental requirements or by its military objectives and demands regarding weapons systems. So the issue is not whether the state exerts an influence, but how it does so, by what means, with what overt or less overt objectives.

We must reach a very broad consensus on these state-set objectives at European level. Obviously, national economic differences lead to different priorities, and obviously we want to keep national competition alive within the common internal market too. But in areas where we share common European aims we should join forces in our industrial or research and technology activity whenever that promises better and more rapid results than national competition.

I will now clarify a few aspects of a European industrial policy, giving priority to the completion of the internal market and its effects on employment and competition policy. I will then comment on research and technology policy and finally turn to what we German Social Democrats regard as the main aim of industrial policy, the ecological renewal of our economy.

COMPLETING THE COMMON INTERNAL MARKET

The new impetus towards finally completing the common market called for even in the Treaties of Rome was certainly spurred on by the worldwide economic recession in the early 1980s and the fears that Europe could not keep up in the technical and economic competition with Japan, the USA and the newly industrialized Asian countries. It was widely put about that Europe had become paralysed, unable to adapt to structural shifts of supply and demand. This had to be countered by a new dynamic impetus – free markets instead of European paralysis.

We may agree or disagree with these views. But there can be no doubt that the completion of the internal market will open new opportunities for the Community's industrial and services sector and that the more productive use of economic resources resulting from stronger competition within Europe will also strengthen the Community's position in international competition.

The European Community now has a population of 320 million, compared with 234 million in the USA and 120 million in Japan. After China and India, it therefore has the third highest population in the world. In 1987 the European Community's GNP was barely 4.2 billion dollars, compared with 4.3 billion in the USA and 2.4 billion in Japan.

It must be the aim of everyone, and the cornerstone of European industrial policy, to make more effective use of this potential source of labour, of inventiveness, of technical knowledge and know-how.

It will still take considerable efforts before we manage to reduce or co-ordinate the border controls in the Community, the technical barriers to trade, the differences between national legal provisions and tax barriers and to achieve the completely free movement of goods, persons, services and capital between the Member States. According to the Commission's White Paper, this will involve adopting 286 individual legislative measures. So far, 100 of these draft laws have been adopted, but the more difficult harmonization measures are still to come. Nevertheless, that is not cause for any doubt about the chances of rapidly completing the internal market.

To begin with, the EC has in many areas moved away from its traditional idea of totally harmonizing national provisions and has finally decided to accept the mutual recognition of national provisions and situations.

Secondly, where Community legislation is absolutely necessary, it is to confine itself to regulating the main objectives and mandatory requirements of the matter in question, leaving most of the detailed technical rules to be worked out by specialist organizations such as the European standards organizations. This will relieve the Community institutions of some of the detailed work and ensure that the economy is not bound by all too far-reaching rules.

Thirdly, the Single European Act has brought about a decisive procedural breakthrough. In future, the majority principle will apply to Council votes in many areas of internal market policy, instead of the unanimity principle which has tended to prevail in the past.

Thanks to these new strategies and procedural provisions, the internal market has now become a realistic prospect, even though in one of the most important and most difficult areas, tax harmonization, there are no signs yet of a solution that is likely to be accepted by all the Member States, as is still required in this exceptional case.

STRENGTHENING COMPETITION AND SECURING IT FOR THE FUTURE

The completion of the internal market means, first and foremost, more competition – more competition on the markets for industrial products, the services markets, more competition for public contracts. The wide divergences sometimes found among the Community countries in the prices of bank services, insurance premiums, transport costs, and in particular goods supplied by state undertakings or private enterprises which more or less have a monopoly, such as telephone exchanges or power stations, make it clear that some sectors have settled themselves comfortably behind the remaining national protective barriers. So there is certain to be resistance to attempts to dismantle these barriers.

It will undoubtedly prove particularly difficult to open up the public contracts system to greater European and non-European competition, not only because national 'purveyors to the Court' have become established, but also because this area often concerns key or forward-looking technologies, such as telecommunications. It is likely that it will remain a matter of national pride in future too for a country to promote the technology of its 'own' undertakings by the award of public contracts and the protection of jobs in those undertakings.

The opening up of the transport market will also involve considerable difficulties. It must go hand in hand with the approximation of conditions of competition. The lower prices for transport by road and by air resulting from the liberalization of these markets will bring Europe closer together, promote trade and increase transport revenues, but it will also strain our transport infrastructure and air space to the limit. For environmental reasons alone we cannot allow that. Instead we must formulate a common European transport policy which will bring about a revival of rail transport and lead to more environmentally compatible and less accident-prone modes of transport.

The completion of the internal market will promote the trend towards mergers between undertakings. A whole wave of such mergers has already become apparent.

Of course the European internal market allows for larger undertakings than in the past, when large size was not compatible with the maintenance of strong competitive structures on the nationally segmented European markets. But we must take preventive measures here, for these large undertakings seek to become larger. Power seeks more power. That is why we must improve European competition law and strengthen the European Community's executive powers in competition policy. There would be no point tearing down national protectionist barriers with a view to creating the internal market while closing one's eyes to the private barriers created by cartel agreements, cooperation arrangements of mergers between undertakings. The effective control of concentrations must assure competition in the long term. Competition is the driving force behind economic and technological performance. Dynamic competition must therefore form the core of any European industrial policy.

KEEPING THE EXTERNAL BORDERS OPEN

That is why we refuse to use the stronger competitive pressure within the European Community which will come with 'Europe 1992' as a pretext for erecting new protective barriers against third countries. First, this would only act as a challenge to other countries to take counter-measures and thus put the European Community's exports to those countries at risk. Secondly, we Europeans are not so weak that we need EC protective tariffs in order to become internationally competitive. This would only undermine our efforts to keep up in the international competitive struggle and tempt us to laziness. Temporary protective tariffs would become permanent tariffs. In the end we would fall even further behind in competition, possibly even in areas in which we are now highly competitive. Europe should become more open to outside competition and look upon the sharper competition on the European market as an incentive and an opportunity to assert its position on the world markets.

PROMOTING STRUCTURAL CHANGE

Competition cannot stop at sectors with structural adjustment problems.

Continuing to preserve outdated structures would be the wrong way to prevent structural change. It would merely prevent the most productive use being made of labour, capital and technical know-how, which is what the efficiency of every national economy depends on.

That is why both national and European industrial policy must be geared to promoting structural change. However, this process must occur in a manner that is both socially and regionally acceptable. If, for example, there is a risk of whole regions becoming depopulated as a result of undertakings closing down or mass redundancies, it is essential to provide prompt help for the provision of alternative jobs and training for the employees.

By European standards, the speed at which large shipyards, steelworks and mines were replaced by new industries in Japan was breathtaking. The close co-operation between state and economy found there may have been a factor. What certainly was decisive was that the undertakings were obliged to create new jobs for their workers, most of whom had been employed there for all their lives. This example also shows that the promotion of structural change certainly does not require American 'hiring and firing' methods. What is far more important is a far-sighted and innovative management that takes its obligations towards its employees seriously and provides continuous further training and vocational training for its employees for increasingly demanding activities.

INVOLVING THE SME'S CLOSELY IN 'EUROPE 1992'

In the beginning, the completion of the internal market will mainly benefit enterprises which are already actively engaged in foreign trade, have linguistically competent staff and the necessary organizational and legal knowledge. These tend to be medium to large firms. But the full effect of the internal market will not be felt until the small and medium-sized enterprises also adjust to the larger market and make use of their opportunities.

The following figures may show the importance of efficient small and medium-sized enterprises to the Federal Republic. SMEs with fewer than 500 employees or a turnover of less than DM 100 million account for about 50% of the German national product and employ 66% of total labour. More than 80% of all employees are trained in SMEs. These small and medium-sized undertakings are responsible for indispensable achievements in the development of technical and economic innovations, opening up future markets and strengthening competition. They also play a decisive role in creating jobs. Surveys in the Federal Republic have shown that as a whole, in recent years the only positive impetus towards employment has come from small undertakings. For instance, the number of workers in undertakings employing up to 49 workers rose by 665,000 between 1977 and 1985. In undertakings with 50 to 499 workers the number employed fell by 26,700; in undertakings with 500 or more workers, it actually fell by 225,000. Whereas some decades ago heavy industry was the key to economic development and job creation, and a few years ago it still looked as though multinationals would form the basis of future prosperity, we now know that the SMEs make a decisive contribution to the continuous renewal of our national economy.

Industrial policy, and economic policy in general, must therefore set itself the aim of involving the SMEs more closely in 'Europe 1992' and informing them about their new opportunities.

DEVELOPING THE EUROPEAN MONETARY SYSTEM

A common European currency would greatly simplify the trade and investment activities of European undertakings. That is why the market forces are already working towards a common currency. The European currency unit, the ECU, is therefore becoming more and more popular. With the agreement to dismantle the remaining capital transaction controls step by step by 1992, there will be even greater pressure to develop the European Monetary System.

We Social Democrats are in favour of the creation of a politically independent European central bank. We are also in favour of the next step: a uniform European currency. A common currency, free trade and free capital transactions would fuse the Member States together into an economic unit which would be in no way inferior to the United States of America. At the same time, given a common currency and large common money and capital markets, we Europeans could create a counterpart to the dollar and the yen and strengthen our monetary power and influence in the world. That would indicate to others that the European countries have come together to form an effective economic and monetary union.

THE INTERNAL MARKET IS NO SUBSTITUTE FOR EMPLOYMENT POLICY

As you know, the Commission presented a broadly based analysis of the effects of the internal market in the Cecchini report. It reaches the conclusion that the dismantling of border formalities, the liberalization of the public contracts and procurement system, the liberalization of financial services and the sharper competition or sudden boom in supply promises to bring economic advantage of 175 to 255 billion ECU for the undertakings. That would correspond to a rise in the Community's national product of 4.25 to 6.5%. The Commission expects consumer prices to fall by an average of at least 6% and the national budgets to benefit from additional tax revenue and cheaper public procurements. In the medium term, 1.8 million new jobs could be created as a result of the completion of the internal market.

The Commission took a further step and examined what could be achieved in terms of employment if the budget appropriations released by stronger growth and lower expenditure were used for an expansive economic policy, tax reliefs or more public investment. In the event that this kind of 'cooperative strategy for growth and employment' is pursued side by side with the achievement of the internal market, the Commission counts on an increase of no less than 5 million jobs in the Community.

In spite of all the necessary reservations via à vis estimates of this kind, they do make two things clear.

First, the completion of the internal market cannot by itself act as a substitute for a job-creation policy on the part of the Community Member States. The probable 1.8 million extra jobs look very modest compared to the figure of 16.7 million officially registered as unemployed in the European Community.

Secondly, the internal market's effect on the employment situation in the Community can be enhanced by an accompanying 'cooperative strategy for growth and employment'. This strategy is essential for several reasons. First and foremost, the short-term job-losses to be expected as a result of the completion of the internal market must be absorbed. Furthermore, the resistance of undertakings and workers to the implementation of the internal market must be weakened by stronger economic growth and the resulting improvement in job prospects. But above all, it would be quite senseless to waste enormous political and economic efforts on strengthening the efficiency of industry and the commercial services sector in the hope of possibly creating 1.8 million new jobs, while at the same time allowing the willingness and ability to work of 15 million unemployed citizens of the European Community go to waste.

EXPANDING THE EUROPEAN INFRASTRUCTURE

There is good reason to believe that the implementation of the internal market will run smoothly if Europe continues in the direction of a general economic growth of about 2 per cent. And it is certain that if this trend continues, it will not be possible to reduce the appallingly high unemployment rate in the Community countries. So Europe must make sustained and combined efforts to launch a private and public investment campaign to create new jobs.

Each country will have its own ideas on how best to achieve this. And the margin for manoeuvre differs from country to country. However, as the Commission rightly keeps pointing out, the opportunities and effects will be all the greater if the European Community states pusue a joint job-creating policy.

Special efforts can no doubt be expected to the Federal Republic in this area. Its economic strength, its trade and current account surpluses enable it to give impetus to the European economy. But we would be defining our objective too narrowly if we said we aimed only at improving economic growth. Growth has no value *per se*. Only if it leads to qualitative improvements, i.e. in particular to more employment in all the European countries, is the effort worth making.

We Social Democrats think the key to more growth and employment in the Federal Republic lies in specific incentives for more private investment, a vocational training campaign for workers and substantial public and private investment to restore our natural environment. These ideas are set out in detail under the heading 'Special assets: labour and the environment'.

Investment activity is both possible and necessary at European level too. The European Community should broaden the European Investment Bank's loan terms in order to create funds for European investment projects. The construction of an additional transport route between Germany and Italy, the development of a high-speed train network, the expansion of European ports, the computerization of telephone networks, the more rapid creation of a European communications and data network are useful productive investments. Such investments would no doubt also give considerable impetus to increased private investment. Coordinated efforts in environmental policy, from saving the North Sea to cleaning up the Mediterranean and the rivers of Europe, could be another major task for the European Community.

FORMULATING A NEW INDUSTRIAL POLICY

Community efforts to strengthen the European infrastructure would also benefit European industrial policy. Just as the USA

99

gave a quite novel impetus to scientific and technical development some 28 years ago when President Kennedy defined the objective of flying to the moon, we Europeans should also define our aims and gear the activities or our economy towards them.

The German Social Democrats' priority social and therefore industrial aim is to achieve products and production methods which are more compatible with natural cycles and preserve the natural bases of our existence. Products and production technologies of this kind will certainly also provide important markets in future, given the global threats to the environment.

It would also be a good idea to encourage the management and staff of undertakings to become more willing to accept and carry out technical and organizational innovations. The workers' anxiety about their vocational skills being devalued by technical innovations must be allayed by offers of continuous and further training. It is important to involve them in the introduction of innovations, to make the workplace humane and to create a climate of mutual trust. In short, people must realise that good working relations are a force for innovation and production.

Larger markets, more competition and the willingness to introduce social innovations will give European industry new impetus for growth. But we cannot rely on that alone. The massive research aid given from the defence budget in the USA and the close cooperation between state and industry in Japan have long since shifted the focus on international competition from the level of the undertaking to state level in many areas. Our ideal is not to see all the nations embark on a techno-mercantile race. But in view of the scale of basic research and large technical projects, we will continue to require substantial public funds to become or remain competitive. As examples I need only mention satellite technology, glass fibre technology, microelectronics, laser technology and genetic research.

I am aware of the difficulties involved here. How much influence should we give to research and technology policy? Is there not a tendency to build up 'forward-looking industries' behind walls protecting them from outside competition? Is there not a risk of being steered in the wrong direction?

Of course there are enough examples of the state showing insufficient foresight or even being an actual failure. But the process of economic and technological development cannot be left to run by itself. We need forecasts. We need supervision by society and the framework must be defined by social and ecological criteria directed not at maximum quantity but at optimum quality. That is why I have no hesitation about formulating definite aims for the benefit of man and nature and creating the framework conditions for directing research and technological development towards the aim of the ecological renewal of our industrial society.

III TOWARDS ECOLOGICAL RENEWAL

GROWING ECOLOGICAL RISKS

The German Social Democratic approach towards the ecological renewal of industrial society which I describe below is not based on any finished theory yet. We are still in the throes of a process of discussion, involved in the reorientation of the principles of our economic policy. The fundamental questions have been resolved, but we have not yet formulated all the details of our approach.

For us, the ecological renewal of the economy does not only mean environmental protection in the narrow sense, it does not just mean a policy on the protection of the species, the protection of the soil, clean air and clean water – for us the ecological renewal of industrial society means bringing the economic process into balance with the cycle of nature, regarding ecology as economics for the long term.

Naturally we regard ecological renewal not as a national but as a global issue. Eleven million hectares of forest are destroyed every year, mainly in the third world. Over a period of 30 years that would represent an area the size of India.

Every year 6 million hectares of usable agricultural land is turned into barren desert.

At the same time more and more toxic substances from industry and agriculture penetrate the human food chain. The burning of fossil fuels is raising the temperature of the earth's atmosphere and creating a global greenhouse effect whose consequences in terms of the rise of the sea-level are still incalculable. Entire coastal regions are now at risk.

Ten years ago the world was caught unawares by the Seveso disaster. All of a sudden we were shown the dangers of chemical production. The accident at the fertilizer factory in Bhopal in India, when more than 2,000 died and more than 200,000 were blinded; the explosion of liquid gas containers in Mexico City when more than 1,000 died; the Rhine disaster in early 1987 when fertilizers, detergents and mercury flowed into the Rhine in Basel and killed off all life in the lower course of the river; the death of the seals in the North Sea: all this was drastic evidence of the dangers of chemical production both in the developing countries and in the highly industrialized countries.

Since the nuclear disaster at Chernobyl we have come to realise how fragile the experts' promises are that a massive disaster is virtually impossible. The risk of wide-scale damage from radioactive radiation, which no one can avoid, is no longer an abstract risk since Chernobyl but has become a life-threatening reality for countless people. The question of the peaceful use of nuclear energy can no longer be put aside simply by saying that every technique entails both risks and opportunities. Nuclear energy is a technology of a fundamentally new type with a fundamentally different risk potential.

TECHNOLOGICAL DEVELOPMENT IS INTEREST-BASED

In its approach to nuclear energy the SPD rejects the old Socialist theory that technological development is an autonomous, value-free process. In our 1959 Godesberg Programme we still said of the peaceful use of nuclear energy that it was not the techniques or the development of productive forces that we should worry about but their use in society. It was the social production relationships which turned forces of production into forces of destruction.

Today our new draft party programme reads: 'Technology is developing at a rate and its potential is expanding to a level for which there are no parallels in history. But technical development is not an autonomous, unalterable process. Technology is interest-based, shaped by value systems, determined largely by its involvement in international competition, dependent on what is known about its consequences. Technology is not neutral in terms of its effect on society. Different techniques have a greater or lesser effect – largely independent of the user's intentions – in terms of environmental pollution, the risk of accidents, safety requirements, the need for centralization and control.'

This fundamentally new approach distinguishes the concept of the ecological renewal of our industrial society from the traditional environmental policy formulated by the SPD at the end of the 1950s. Willy Brandt had introduced the subject of the environment into the political debate as early as 1961 with his electoral slogan 'Blue skies over the Ruhr'. In the 1960s, 'environmental protection' was still perceived as a political problem. It was left to the Social-Liberal coalition of the early 1970s to introduce a whole range of draft laws and try to make up for what had not been done in the 1950s and 1960s. But it was the major environmental disasters of the 1970s and early 1980s that led us to decide a fundamental change of course.

OUR AIMS

I have already pointed out that we regard ecological renewal as an all-embracing political concept covering all areas of life: production, working life, consumption and leisure. Our aims are as follows:

- To achieve structural change in order to replace environmentally harmful forms of production and consumption with environmentally compatible ones.
- To promote technical innovation with a view to new techniques that can make production processes and products more environment-friendly.
- To take comprehensive disposal measures to eliminate dangerous pollutants as far as possible.
- To eliminate the long-term pollutants of our environment, which go back over 150 years of industrial history.

I would like to clarify our view of ecological renewal by three examples. First, we want to use the special assets of 'labour and the environment' to eliminate the long-term pollutants from our environment and at the same time to give impetus to the development of environment-friendly technologies. Second, by formulating a forward-looking chemicals policy we want to defuse the risks arising from chemical production and products.

Third, on the basis of our non-nuclear energy policy, we want to switch over to safer and environmentally compatible energy supplies that do not use nuclear energy.

SPECIAL ASSETS: LABOUR AND THE ENVIRONMENT

Investment in the environment is a profitable investment, not for the individual undertaking but for the economy as a whole. Surveys have shown that today an effective investment of one billion in the environment can produce an annual profit of at least 25,000 million in the form of damage that has been avoided. That is far higher than the profit the economy could gain from transport investment for instance.

The experts estimate the fall in the standard of living due to environmental pollution at 3 to 6 per cent of GNP a year. At the same time the Federal Republic spends a mere 2 per cent a year on environmental measures. So in terms of size, the annual damage resulting from failure to protect the environment is far greater than the cost of preserving our environment. Seen in purely economic terms, it is entirely in our interests to invest in a cleaner environment.

Just as we managed to rebuild our country after the war and to tackle the housing shortage by a major community effort, so today we see it as a political task to protect the environment and remove any damage that has already occurred.

In order to help reduce unemployment at the same time, we have proposed another major community effort under the heading 'Special assets: labour and the environment'. In the next ten years an additional sum of about DM 20 billion a year is to be allocated to investment in environmental projects which would otherwise have been postponed or dropped for lack of funds.

The aid programme concentrates on measures to improve the protection of the water and of water supplies, in the waste disposal industry, to keep the air clean, to use energy more rationally and economically, to protect nature and the landscape, and in urban ecology.

The very title 'Special assets: labour and the environment' shows that we want to help overcome mass unemployment. Careful model analyses by various economic research institutes have shown that annual environmental investments of DM 20,000 could provide jobs for up to 400,000 people.

TOWARDS A POLICY ON THE CHEMICAL INDUSTRY

The history of human civilization is the history of the mastery and transformation of nature through labour. We obtain substances from the natural environment and transform them into higher-grade products. During the phase of industrialization in the last 200 years, attention focussed mainly on production. It tended to be forgotten too often that the natural substances we have appropriated must be returned to the environment – as waste, sewage and gases.

No one denies that the achievements of the natural sciences and technology have bestowed upon us the immense wealth

105

which we have now acquired, at least in the industrialized countries. But we have only just realised that intensive use of natural substances entails serious risks for man, the animal world and the environment.

So we need to take an overall view, a uniform approach to a policy on the chemical industry that is acceptable in both environmental and health terms. We have formulated such an overall approach in the past few years. The kind of preventive policy on chemicals we support inquires into the usefulness of chemical products to man, i.e. is concerned with their social and economic net utility. It evaluates the positive and negative effects of substances, including the corresponding side-products and processed products, during their production, utilization and disposal. A preventive policy on the chemical industry aims at the responsible use of chemicals, which means:

- Using fewer resources in production.
- The least possible harm to the employees and to the environment during the production process.
- Developing products whose use and disposal involves as few health and environmental risks as possible.

Responsibility for avoiding and removing chemical substances which entail health and environmental risks must lie with the undertaking. It is not the task of the state to anticipate the investment decisions of private undertakings. But it is the task of the state to protect public health. It must do so by laying down a clear, strict legal framework setting out the conditions for the utilization of nature and the environment, in the form of instructions, levies, rules and prohibitions, and following 'the polluter pays' principle.

NUCLEAR-FREE ENERGY POLICY

At the 1986 Nuremberg party congress the SPD decided on a change of policy on energy after nearly ten years of difficult discussions. For the first time in its history the party was faced with the question of how to beat an orderly retreat from a highly developed technology because of the impossibility of overcoming the dangers and risks it involved. Conscious of its historical responsibility towards future generations, the SPD decided it was no longer justifiable to expose the public to the dangers and risks involved in the use of nuclear power even for civil purposes. That is why the Nuremberg party congress formulated a nuclear-free energy policy for the Federal Republic of Germany. It provides for the rapid transition to a safe, environmentally acceptable energy policy that protects our natural resources. We realised that the implementation of such a radical decision requires a legislative majority in the parliaments.

Our policy of nuclear-free energy supplies forms part of our programme for the ecological renewal of industrial society. The reform of our energy system involves four requirements:

1. To save energy.
2. To avoid and reduce environmental pollution wherever possible.
3. To make renewable energy sources the main components of the future energy system.
4. To leave our descendants their freedom of decision and to predetermine their way of life as little as possible.

We take the view that it is more advantageous both for the environment and for the economy to invest in energy-saving techniques and renewable energy sources than to widen the range of energy supplies. Since the 1973/1974 oil crisis we in the Federal Republic have been very successful in increasing energy productivity thanks to concerted action by the state, industry and the consumer. Between 1973 and 1985 our GNP rose by 24 per cent in real terms, while energy consumption rose by only 2.5 per cent. We consider it possible, without any fall in standards of living, to save up to 50% in domestic heat, 10% in industrial-process heat and 20% in electricity in the next ten years.

In the long term we will be able to cover our energy demand

only if we develop solar energy, wind energy, water power and the biomass as energy sources. Everyone knows that the fossil fuels oil, gas and coal are limited. That is why it is particularly important today to develop the renewable energy sources in the next ten to twenty years. It would be mistaken to expect renewable energy sources to have any real potential as primary energy sources in this century. But we must formulate a long-term research, industry and energy policy now to pave the way for energy supplies which can replace nuclear power and fossil fuels in the next century.

This readjustment can be supported and speeded up by further developments in the tax system. At its party congress in Münster in September 1988 the SPD decided to expand the tax and levy system to include an ecological component. The preservation of the natural bases of our standard of living is added to the traditional aims of tax policy. The use of scarce resources and non-renewable energy sources is to be taxed higher and therefore reduced. Similarly, environmentally harmful production processes will become more expensive, which will inhibit them. The additional tax revenue this produces can be used for tax reliefs for small and medium incomes. But it can also be used specifically for the creation of new jobs, for example by making the labour factor cheaper or by financing environmental investments. The 'Special asset: labour and the environment' we proposed should thus be financed by an additional tax on energy consumption.

To summarize: The concept of the ecological renewal of industrial society is a programme embracing every aspect of human life. It is the blueprint for a society that respects the natural law of global ecological balance, which cannot be infringed without the risk of disastrous consequences. We must learn to produce, to distribute and to consume in such a way as to leave nature intact and preserve the natural bases of human life. We must realise that man is not the measure of all things but that man is himself part of nature. The environmental disasters of recent decades have reminded us of that age-old awareness. To make that the starting point for our thoughts and actions today does not mean going 'back to nature' or 'rejecting industrial society', it means bringing man's economic activity into harmony with the laws of nature.

The ecological renewal of industrial society is a challenge to human creativity; it is a challenge to scientists and technicians to study and develop environmentally compatible production methods and products; it is a challenge to undertakings, management and unions to steer the innovation and investment process in that direction; it is a challenge to the state to set out a well-defined system of ecological rules for the utilization of nature and to speed up the process of renewal by offering economic incentives; it is a challenge to social groups to make man more keenly aware of ecological questions. Last but not least, ecological renewal is a challenge to Europe to exercize its powers to protect and preserve the environment.

IV THE EUROPE OF SOCIAL DEMOCRACY

'Europe 1992' has awakened forces which will keep the process of integration moving. Lack of political courage, provincial attitudes, the clinging to national sovereign rights and the fears of strong economic groups that there will be 'too much' competition will always impede that movement.

So the European process of integration will remain an arduous one. But it can no longer be stopped. We German Social Democrats want Europe. Throughout the 125 years of our party's history we and all the European forces of Social Democracy have always stood for international understanding and cooperation. Even in our 1925 Heidelberg party programme we declared our aim to be the 'United States of Europe'. The Social Democratic parties of Europe have given strong impetus to the creation of the European Community and its development. We shall continue to strive to ensure that the European Parliament obtains the rights of participation which the national parliaments have long since lost in many areas of European policy-making.

Europe must become a Europe of social democracy. That means:
1. Industrial peace and social welfare in Europe.
2. Economic and ecological renewal in Europe.
3. A democratic Europe.
4. A peaceful Europe which uses its economic and political influence, its spiritual traditions and historical experiences to ensure peaceful cooperation between nations.